EDUCATION for DIGNITY

EDUCATION for DIGNITY

Marianne Frostig, Ph.D.

Founder, Executive Director Emeritus, and Director of Research Projects
The Marianne Frostig Center of Educational Therapy
and Professor of Education
Mount St. Mary's College
Los Angeles, California

GRUNE & STRATTON
A Subsidiary of Harcourt Brace Jovanovich, Publishers
New York   San Francisco   London

Library of Congress Cataloging in Publication Data

Frostig, Marianne.
  Education for dignity.

  Includes bibliographical references and index.
  1. Handicapped children—Education. I. Title.
LC4015.F76   371.9   76-25151
ISBN 0-8089-0951-7

Grune & Stratton, Inc.
111 Fifth Avenue
New York, New York 10003

Distributed in the United Kingdom by
Academic Press, Inc. (London) Ltd.
24/48 Oval Road, London NW 1

Library of Congress Catalog Card Number 76-25151
International Standard Book Number 0-8089-0951-7
Printed in the United States of America

CONTENTS

ACKNOWLEDGMENTS

It would be impossible for me to identify all the many friends, co-workers, scientists, and philosophers who have influenced my writings, engendered new ideas, and helped directly and indirectly with the work on this book.

But there are some who stand out among all those who assisted me. First I must thank my co-worker, Phyllis Maslow, whose criticism and editing has been of the greatest help. Another co-worker, David Horne, has helped with the editing of some of the chapters and gone through the pages with a fine toothed comb to check on any Germanisms, most unwelcome reminders of my childhood that have a tendency to creep into the text. Phyllis Gedge, my secretary of many years, has interrupted her well-earned retirement to assist with the typing. The always helpful Ellen Takahashi has managed to help, too, by squeezing extra typing into her busy work schedule. Barbara Bozman was always able to retrieve references which seemed to elude me and has been always patient and kind when I needed her help. And Freda Shapiro helped in many ways to enliven flagging spirits with a cup of coffee and a friendly word, in addition to performing numerous tasks which saved my time for writing.

Two assistants contributed to the text of this book. Ann-Marie Miller was the original author of the description of the Hartford Project, in which she was a supervising teacher. Denise Jakeman Nighman's charming and witty ways, as well as her efficiency and competency, helped to get the complete cooperation of the Compton public school personnel and thereby assured the success of that project.

I therefore extend to these co-workers not only my thanks but also my warmest friendship and sincerest admiration for their dedication.

INTRODUCTION

Children of these and times to come are lucky because so many persons genuinely care about their growth and learning, about their welfare and nurturance, and about their lives in the present and in the future.

The author of this book is a keen, humane champion of all children, and her philosophy is made real, beautiful, and totally useful in this volume. As one who has known and admired Marianne Frostig for many years, I feel that she truly walks in and out of the valuable pages of this book. She will have a special impact on the reader just as she has had impact on so many young lives.

As one reads *Education for Dignity,* one becomes aware that for Dr. Frostig all children are special and have special needs. There are educationally handicapped children, minority children, unloved children, abused children, cross-culturally imported children, parentless children, overactive children —all of them need special caring and help to grow into and flourish as happy, healthy, and productive adults. They need help that is individually structured and given; they need help as members of small and larger groups. Such help can be given in humane, creative, and growth-producing ways, whether one is teaching art, music, dance, language, science, mathematics, or human behavior skills. The focus of this book is on the philosophy and realistic ways of translating into practice teaching–learning transactions that will have impact on and meaning for each child exposed to the educational process and persons.

Finding meaning in life depends in part on successful searches for meaning by every person, both young and old.* The author suggests many ways in which the helping adult can enhance the child's search for a healthy self-image and a meaningful life. Sometimes this is done through direct, encouraging, creative help; sometimes through the modeling behavior of the adult; sometimes through the methods and media utilized.

All adults interested in and involved with children will find this a useful and inspirational volume, whether they are educators, teacher aides, school volunteers, social workers, parents, psychologists, pediatricians, child

---

*Schindler-Rainman E, Lippitt R: Our Searches for Meaning Today. Los Angeles, The California Museum of Science and Industry, 1976.

psychiatrists, clergy, religious educators, or recreationists. It is a significant support for those who give energy and commitment to children with special needs.

It is a book to be read, enjoyed, and used. There are many ways that this could happen: through reading and small discussion groups; by using suggested ideas and adapting them and then sharing them among colleagues; by selecting particular parts (e.g., art education or creative activities), reading them, and then reporting on them and discussing them with a view to trying them in practice; and through support among colleagues for trying something new with accompanying feedback and possibilities for revision and adaptation, as well as continued support.

Humane ideas such as those presented in this book deserve every effort we can make to convert them into humane actions for our children. This is what *Education for Dignity* demands and deserves.

Eva Schindler-Rainman, DSW

FOREWORD

In *Education for Dignity,* Dr. Frostig has brought into clearer focus the science and art of teaching as it must relate to the goals of education in the last quarter of this century.

There is more a concern about rather than a zest for the future. Although technology has enabled man to walk on the moon, he still advances with faltering steps here on earth. The values of the past remain to be reconciled with the changing values of the future. Institutions of government, church, family, and school are being challenged as never before. All these problems notwithstanding, the belief persists that institutions can be changed to meet the demands of our time. It is evident that the institutions of the school will serve a primary role in helping people to cope with those problems that threaten their survival.

Students of educational philosophy will note that we have come into a period of testing the use of the school as an instrument to facilitate social change. Laws are written and court rulings applied to assure equal opportunity, equal protection, and due process in assuring a person his or her rights as an individual as well as a member of a group. It is believed that laws and court rulings alone cannot assure freedom, truth, and justice. Such ideals can be attained only by an enlightened and moral people. Education is the means by which people become enlightened and moral. In the final analysis, education is preparation for the good life as it should apply to all mankind.

Certain realities confront us as we look to the future. The bounties of nature are rich but not limitless. We must now learn to conserve rather than exploit, replenish what we diminish, and recycle what can be reused. Technological changes will contine at their rapid pace and to some extent help to solve the problems they create. The problems of impacted societies —urbanization—will continue to challenge us as there is less and less space for more and more people. The family unit will struggle for survival. There will be the continued search for the worthwhile, for the credible, for the valid, and for the secure things in life. In the balance, the major concerns of this last quarter of the twentieth century relate to people problems rather than material resources.

People problems can be solved because people can be changed through education. Dr. Frostig has devoted her life to the premise that each individual learner is important as a person. He or she must be understood as a person. In accordance with the natural order of human growth and development, an individual plan can be formulated to foster skills, knowledge, human relationships, self-realization, and moral values which will assure the kind of security needed for continued growth toward maturity. Although behavior can be shaped, the teacher as a model will seek to draw out or nurture that kind of appropriate behavior which the individual explores and discovers for himself. The essence of individualization is respect for the individual. The moral lesson of respect for the child by the classroom teacher constitutes the most profound model that a school can provide in helping society attain that which is most needed at this time—a true concern and regard for the general welfare of all mankind. *Education for Dignity* takes the reader beyond the usual parameters of pedagogy and reminds all of us that we learn to become that which can make life most meaningful for ourselves and others.

Ernest P. Willenberg
Assistant Superintendent
Division of Special Education
Los Angeles City Schools

PREFACE

A few words are necessary to describe how this book came about. It is an outgrowth of lectures given in Brisbane, Sydney, Melbourne, and Perth during my second trip to Australia in 1972. So much interest was shown in such topics as ability training, classroom management, educational diagnosis, and creative teaching and learning that I decided to try to put my views and comments into book form.

Unfortunately, my work load delayed the volume's completion, and in the time that has since passed so many changes have taken place that much had to be rewritten. For example, in 1972 the extension of the European Common Market seemed to promise a prosperous future for Europe. International safeguards for nuclear-powered weaponry seemed about to be forged. The "green revolution" seemed to promise food for the people of overpopulated countries. Only four years later in 1976 the economies of many countries are in serious straits, effective international agreements regarding arms control seem impossible to achieve (we seem unable even to regulate arms in our own country), and the "green revolution" has proved to be a failure, at least temporarily. The Watergate affair and reports of wrongdoing in the CIA arouse feelings of abhorrence, anger, and guilt. Thus it seems even more essential that our children be involved in an education that truly fits them to deal creatively with the moral and practical issues with which they will eventually be confronted.

Only those topics that reflect the current struggle of educators to achieve these ends have been included in this volume. The teaching of academic skills has been treated in more detail in a companion volume, *Learning Problems in the Classroom.** There is some overlap between the two books in the chapter on assessment. This was necessary to permit the reader unfamiliar with *Learning Problems in the Classroom* to obtain a well-rounded account of specific educational problems with which the teacher is confronted. The account here is more detailed, however, and includes examples of analyses of test patterns, of the application of test results, and of case histories.

*Published by Grune & Stratton, New York, in 1973.

Although this book deals with some aspects of education for all children, it is especially pertinent to the education of children who seem unable to fit into the traditional school, either because they lag in abilities that enable learning to take place without difficulty or because they are unhappy, emotionally disturbed, or ill-prepared.

This book is intended as a practical guide for the teacher working in the regular classroom, for the teacher of children with special educational needs, and for school psychologists and clinical psychologists interested in educational problems. It is also a textbook for students, social workers, sociologists, and school nurses.

The basic philosophy it expresses is that no education can be effective if it is not adapted to the needs of the children, the present needs of society, and the needs of mankind in the future. If the needs of the children are not satisfied, their development will be stunted; if the needs of the present society are not satisfied, education will not make a positive impact on contemporary life; and if the needs of the future are not taken into account, mankind may not survive or will do so only in a debased manner.

It is hoped that the present work will help educators, potential educators, and guidance personnel to respond effectively to the issues with which education must currently be concerned. We who work with children have a large responsibility. In nurturing and teaching them, we influence not only the future of individual children but also the future of human society as a whole.

PART I

Education in an Endangered World

Introduction

Not everything that exists is evident. Nor can everything that exists be explained.

The warning of a Mayan priest

Konrad Lorenz [1] has identified forces that he feels are driving mankind toward disaster. Among them are overpopulation, despoliation of the natural environment, technology developing too rapidly for man to control, substitution of "fun" or superficial pleasures for the deep joy provided by meaningful living, inability to tolerate anything disagreeable—even the slightest loss of comfort—and the disruption of traditional values. These are problems that obviously cannot be solved in a single generation.

The survival of mankind, therefore, depends on developing in ourselves and in our children different values and attitudes. It is no longer sufficient to be able to postpone gratification for the sake of one's own future; broad masses of people must renounce gratification for the sake of future generations. The inhabitants of some developed countries will have to learn to lessen accustomed indulgences in food, possessions, and other pleasures so that the world's limited resources will be more carefully husbanded and more equally shared. People must learn to curb aggressive impulses that harm others and to channel them toward constructive ends.

With these needs in mind, an education that is restricted to teaching the "three Rs" is clearly insufficient. Fundamentals are important, but in responding to the stresses of our time, education is almost being forced to adopt infinitely wider aims. In a world in which events in one remote area can

3

What lies ahead for our children? (Photo by James Quinn and Michael Campa.)

drastically affect what happens all over the globe, in which natural resources are fast vanishing, in which the pressing of a few buttons can annihilate millions and destroy civilization—in such a world only the person who is able to think in global terms for the benefit of mankind as a whole and who devotes herself or himself to the solution of common problems can really be termed "educated."

In this time of change the only prediction about the future that we can make with certainty is that the rate of change will continue to accelerate. Thus, effective adaptation to the demands of the present and future are necessary. This adaptation requires that children be helped to develop the kinds of attitudes and skills that foster the ability to develop creativity and lead to the perception of essential problems and the discovery of more effective methods in solving them.

REFERENCE

1. Lorenz K: Die acht Todsunden der zivilisierten Menschheit. Munich, Ger, Piper, 1973

1
The Purposes of Education

Our schools will have to become places where human beings are valued
for their humanity and not just at best for their intelligence.

L. F. Neal [1]

The forms and goals of the education of any group have to be understood in
relation to both its past history and its present customs and circumstances
because education is always a transmitter of culture and thus subservient to it.
The content of education is selected from the accumulated fund of knowledge,
according to what is regarded as important and valuable for the culture's
well-being and survival.

As cultures change, educational scope and content changes. Yet the most
important goals of education have remained the same throughout human history
because they satisfy essential human needs.

EDUCATION FOR SURVIVAL

The primary goal of any culture or social group is its survival.* Education,
therefore, must ensure that members of a culture know how to procure the
necessities for living, how to defend themselves against natural enemies, and
how to live together peacefully.

Education in this most basic sense of survival predates homo sapiens.

*B. F. Skinner makes this the overriding purpose of education in *Beyond Freedom and
Dignity* [2].

5

Many mammals slap, push, kick, or bite their young whenever the young endanger themselves or scare away prey. Whether through experiential learning or through protection by adults until maturation occurs, or both, the young of many species learn to identify nourishing foods, to find water, to hunt, to establish territory and migratory routes, to mate, and to defend themselves. As animals progress in the phylogenetic scale, the means by which survival is made possible become more diversified. As a consequence, the methods of bringing up the young also become more diversified.

The lower primates may be credited with emphasizing the first great innovation in educational methodology—modeling. Young primates are educated not primarily by punishment and restriction, but by imitation of adult models.* For example, they learn by imitation to use a stick to dig for insects, to make a nest of branches, and to assume social roles according to sex and age [4,5]. In the schools of the 1970s modeling is also an essential educational tool.

"Survival" to modern man, however, has implications unknown to animals and even to mankind up to the last few decades. We live in an overpopulated world of speedily shrinking natural resources. We also live in a world in which man has forged instruments for his own cataclysmic destruction. We are all threatened, and we are all interdependent. It is imperative, therefore, that our children learn to regard themselves as members of a world community—a world community that cannot function smoothly or safely, or even survive, without the cooperative efforts of all its members, whatever their race, religion, education, or socioeconomic level may be. Our children have to understand that cooperation is a biological necessity that applies to any community of animals, whether they are members of a pack of wolves, an ant heap, or a tribe of baboons. But the wolves in Siberia, the ants in one's own backyard, and the baboons in Africa live in their ecological niche without being concerned with living beings on other continents. This is not the case with homo sapiens. The community in which a child lives is influenced by the conditions in his or her country, and the conditions in that country depend on the conditions in other countries. On a practical level, as well as a philosophical one, every nation is interdependent with every other.

Before everything else, the child has to learn that perceived differences between his own ingroup and those outside it must not lead to rejection and feelings of fear and hostility. The child must learn to interact in a friendly and mutually helpful way with newcomers to his or her neighborhood and with those who differ in national, ethnic, racial, or religious characteristics or who have a different life style. A child must learn to understand that those desig-

---

*Harry Harlow's notable work with rhesus monkeys [3] shows clearly that subtle interactions among members of a species are essential for normal growth and survival and not merely, as he had at first hypothesized, for the satisfaction of physical needs.

nated as "enemies," whether by his immediate circle of peers or his govern-ment, are also human beings. He must also learn that the deaths, injuries, and deprivations of others are his concern even if the victim holds the passport of another country, is of another political or religious persuasion, or belongs to another clique just down the street.

In addition, children, and adults too, must be educated to be concerned for the welfare of future generations. For the first time in human history the extinction of mankind looms as a real possibility. Man's greed and ignorance today threaten the basic conditions for life itself. Today, every man, woman, and child must learn the necessity of ecological ethics, of recognizing the dependence of mankind on the earth's resources, and of foregoing immediate surplus gratifications for the sake of those coming after in the chain of life.

EDUCATION FOR SATISFYING THE NEED FOR KNOWLEDGE AND SKILLS

The second main purpose of education, as ancient as the need to ensure survival, and with a most varied history, is the teaching of skills and knowledge that help to make life more secure, more comfortable, and more satisfying. Advances in the use of tools, for example, have been accompanied by the need for more education. Learning to use a digging stick may be viewed as learning to extend one's own body so that food procurement may be easier and more reliable. Viewed this way, the digging stick, the steel ploughshare, and the diesel tractor are steps along a continuum. Moreover, as social and economic roles have gradually become more diversified, educational content has neces-sarily had to become more specialized and more complex.

The beginning of this process can be found in the animal kingdom, as Jane Goodall's observations show [4]. For human beings the specialization of training started with the roles assumed by different members of the tribe and took the form of apprenticeship; a young person worked with a skilled weaver or potter or medicine man or priest to learn the particular "trade." In the modern West education of this kind is still very important, as exemplified by the apprenticeship programs of trade unions, the use of understudies in the per-forming arts, and the internship programs for teachers and physicians.

Progress in specialization has required individualization. Not every member of the tribe could be equally successful as a medicine man or as a hunter, as a herdsman or as a warrior. Even in relatively primitive societies education is adjusted to the capabilities of the individual.

With the advent of written communication, schools were developed to teach reading, writing, and arithmetic. Their teaching has always been a prime function of schools, although the purposes for teaching these skills have varied from age to age. In Puritan New England, for example, reading was valued because it enabled men to receive the word of God. In most homes today reading is more likely to be used for entertainment or gaining information. It is also a necessity for the everyday business of the modern world. Universal compulsory school attendance is mandated in an ever increasing number of countries not only because of humanitarian and political considerations, but also because the close economic and social interdependence of people in the modern world requires written communication.

Thus, modern education must attempt to satisfy personal and societal needs for skills and knowledge of an immense range and in widely varying circumstances.

EDUCATION FOR SATISFYING THE NEED FOR EXPLORATION, CREATIVITY, AND SELF-REALIZATION

The educational goal of learning skills and knowledge necessary for survival, comfort, and security stems from man's organic functions. Additional major educational goals stem from the refinement of man's representational functions and from his ability to use imagery and language to represent events, to form concepts, to formulate ideals, and to perceive relationships not present to his senses. These are characteristics that make us truly human. Although they too are rooted in early phylogenetic development, they have developed to a high degree in humans only. Education must concern itself with their development because they are necessary for exploration, creativity, and self-realization as well as for promoting satisfying interpersonal relationships and group integration.

Representational functions are also necessary so that the achievements of human beings can be transmitted to future generations and developed to a higher degree, especially ethical and moral values. These goals will be discussed in turn.

The Need of the Child for Exploration and Play

Most goals of education are equally important for all human beings, but there are some especially that are the birthright of all children. In particular, education should foster and satisfy the need of a child for exploration and explorative play. Animals also have this basic need. Both young animals and healthy uninhibited children tend to be active, always doing things, exploring, and finding new ways to master the environment. Animals push objects and turn them; they dig without purpose; they jump and chase their shadows and each other. Children can be busy for hours building sand castles; collecting things, arranging them, rearranging them, taking them apart, and putting them together; and finding out about their own abilities by playing together. Play is important for both animals and humans for gaining knowledge about the world around them. The work of Harlow and his associates [3] has convincingly demonstrated the existence of curiosity and a drive toward exploration in monkeys, and similar drives can easily be observed in animals further down the evolutionary scale.

Jean Piaget [6] believes that the search for knowledge is a necessary extension of organic function. The world of a child or adult without the opportunity to exercise his or her natural curiosity is restricted. The individual in such a setting is not participating in an "ever increasing extension of the environment" [6, p 350].

Education, then, must satisfy the child's intrinsic drive to know and to master the environment through the provision of play and work in an atmosphere that encourages exploration. A child who feels that only passive obedience is required of him becomes apathetic or angry, and if he is made to learn that which is not significant to him, his curiosity can become stifled. But if he is encouraged to find out about the world around him and to relate his findings to what he already knows, his joy in learning is delightful and infectious and the fine line between work and play is erased. For example, a group of eight-year-olds in an elementary school started on a nature walk. They did not get far in terms of distance covered, for they stopped 2 feet from the door of their classroom to investigate some crabgrass that had grown through a crack in the cement sidewalk. Their enthusiasm for finding the major root, in measuring the runners (average length, 20 inches!), in noting where new roots were appearing, and so on resulted in bustling activity and in much learning.

Exploration is not only part of child's play. The wish to know propels mankind forward. The lessons of history illustrate this fact. The great explorations of the globe during the fifteenth and sixteenth centuries, the conquests of formerly inaccessible mountains, the probing of subterranean caverns, prodigious journeys beneath the oceans and into outer space, and the monuments of man's intellectual and artistic efforts bear witness to the human need for exploration, for knowledge, and for self-realization and cannot be ascribed solely to materialistic motives.

The desire to explore the unknown and to see and experience something new also contribute to mass movements of population. Today major segments of the population move from city to city, from country to country, from continent to continent; as a consequence the globe seems to be covered with restlessly migrating people. Recreational travel, made possible by economic surplus and high-speed transportation, has also been increasing. Migrations have been, and are, triggered by famine, natural disasters, political and economic repression, and the dangers of war, but certainly the mobility of the population within the United States is not merely a matter of economics.

The need to explore, which is akin to the need for varied stimulation and newness and expresses the need for action, may degenerate or become perverted if a person is confined, whether in a ghetto, in a small apartment or room, or in an educational establishment that fails to stimulate and satisfy the individual's natural urge for physical and mental exploration.

The relevance of exploration to education is fourfold. First, employing the child's need to explore is an important teaching method; exploring makes the child an active participant in the learning process. The teacher should not merely provide the students with an enumeration of facts but should show them how to acquire necessary information for themselves and then how to reformulate and use it.

Second, the active participation of the children keeps them attentive, alert, interested, and delighted with their discoveries.

Third, exploration develops the interests of the teacher and assists the instructor in adapting the curriculum, which is a continuous process necessitated by the constant accumulation of knowledge. For example, who thought of discussing problems connected with space travel or the biochemistry of genetics in regular elementary schools even 10 years ago? Thus not only the children but the teachers too must be active learners.

Fourth, in exploring the outside world, we also explore how we feel about it; thus the child and the teacher are guided in the exploration of their own feelings and attitudes and their own ideas and thoughts and learn to express them. Without the opportunity to explore the affective as well as the intellectual life of the child becomes distorted and repressed. A child will feel more secure, less baffled by the many new and strange occurrences in his life, if he knows how to clarify and express his feelings and communicate his ideas. Without interested and sympathetic adults and peers he will feel shut off from his own feelings, will not be able to appreciate the feelings of others, and will not become aware of what is beautiful and joyful in life. He may learn instead to accept passively his self-centeredness and isolation as a hopeless normality; or he may give vent to repressed feelings in acts of destruction or self-destruction.

Creativity in Education

Creativity builds on exploration. Both are forms of search; both require inventiveness, imagination, and a spirit of inquiry; and both lead to discovery. However, there are also differences between exploration and creativity that make it necessary to consider each separately.

While exploration is always concerned with the physical environment, creativity—although rooted in the concrete world—goes beyond it. Creative experiences are those in which a new relationship is found among previously known elements [7,8].

All human beings have the potential to delight in the discovery of new and unexpected relationships. The infant may discover a relationship between seeing and grasping an object; the astronomer may discover a relationship between time, matter, and energy; and the poet, too, expresses unexpected relationships ("Shall I compare thee to a summer's day?" Shakespeare asks his beloved in his eighteenth sonnet).

The good teacher is also creative. He or she furthers the formation of associations by discovering, or encouraging the discovery of, hidden relationships in the subject matter, thus enhancing both his or her own as well as the child's ability, interest, and enjoyment in exploration and innovation. Let us return to our crabgrass example to illustrate this. The teacher might suggest that the children measure crabgrass runners in different locations. This may lead to the realization that the longest runners occur in loose soil rather than clay, and that they grow close to water sprinklers. The children might then perceive relationships that are new to them and formulate ideas about plant growth and nutrition. After such a discovery, the teacher may encourage the children to express their ideas graphically or verbally or through painting or music.

Self-realization through Education

If a child is involved in creative and explorative activities, he will advance in self-realization: he will feel, "I can discover the world and I can create my own."

The intimate relationship between creativity and self-realization has been beautifully stated by the composer Aaron Copland:

> To the first question—the need to create—the answer is always the same—self-expression; the basic need is to make evident one's deepest feelings about life. But why is the job never done? Why must one always begin again? The reason for the compulsion to renewed creativity, it seems to me, is that each added work brings with it an element of self-discovery. I must create in order to know myself, and since self-knowledge is a never-ending search, each new work is only a part-answer to the question, "Who am I?" and brings with it the need to go on to other and different part-answers. [9, p 233]

Creativity and the Need for Beauty

The needs to explore and express oneself in play and work are not the only mainsprings of creativity. Man also wants to create beauty. Feeling, knowing, and enjoying beauty have always been human needs. Without the understanding of and love for beauty no person can be really human, and no civilization can exist for long without satisfying these needs.

The need for beauty is expressed universally. The aborigines in Australia carve and paint their simple tools or burn designs into the wood; they ornament their sparse clothing with feathers or shells; and they use earthen colors to paint their bodies. The hard-working Indians who live in the high isolated valleys of the Andes of South America, the Mayan peasants who live in the jungles of Yucatan, the poor Polish peasants in the forest-enclosed valleys of the Carpathian Mountains, or the Tartars in the Asian steppes have all developed their own art forms. In the jungles of Africa live the Bambara, who do highly intricate carvings, and the Beni, whose metal work often rivals the most beautiful Western modern art. The Moroccans have developed many of their native crafts to perfection, using metal, leather, tile, cloth, glass, and precious stones. In New Zealand the manifold crafts of the Maori, as well as their songs and dances, command our admiration. In Europe the beauty of churches, peasant cabins, furniture, tools, and utensils rival the beauty of the landscape. Folk songs and dances and religious music are important in everyday life in all countries.

Arts and crafts, music and dance, poetry and epic tales have been, and always must be, a major part of human education because they provide various ways in which the creative drive may be fulfilled and the human need for aesthetic and spiritual satisfaction refined and satisfied. They stimulate the discovery of new relationships among diverse forms and emotions, encourage self-expression and self-discovery, and help to bind the individual to his culture by aiding him in going beyond his own ego needs.

Opportunities for creative self-expression should no longer be regarded as an expendable frill in education; they should be considered as a major part of the curriculum. It should be added that the appearance of the classroom should also be as beautiful as possible—not only because it fosters the children's enjoyment of beauty, but also because it has been found that children work better and more happily in attractive surroundings.

EDUCATION FOR SATISFYING THE NEED FOR HUMAN RELATIONSHIPS

Separation of human needs is never possible in reality. The goals of education discussed thus far all contribute to the goal of social integration.

To be fully human means to respect and care for other persons. It means to feel compassion for others even if they differ in language, customs, or skin color or if they live on the other side of the world. It means to extend oneself in the service of others. Such contacts do not benefit the recipient only; extension of help and kindness is itself a human need. Companionship depends upon a reciprocal giving and taking, with pleasure in both.

Fig. 1-1.   Enjoying a folk tale together. (Photo by James Quinn and Michael Campa.)

People are social beings. They usually experience isolation as very pain-
ful, which is why solitary confinement constitutes such a severe form of
punishment or coercion. Thus children who feel unaccepted by their group and
have difficulties in forming warm and friendly relationships become severely
disturbed; on the other hand, satisfactory contacts with playmates may ameliorate emotional disturbances. Harry Harlow's ''monkey paradise'' demonstrated
that young monkeys who had become neurotic as a result of separation from the
mother could be brought back to an apparently normal, happy life when put
with playmates in a secure and relatively unrestricted environment [10]. The
open classroom structure described in Chapter 5 shows how a teacher-centered
environment can be replaced by a classroom in which the children join cooperatively in common tasks, rely a great deal on each other, and have both the
freedom and the motivation to form friendships. One of the benefits of such a
structure is that the children form closer and happier relationships with the
teachers as well as with each other. Children who are educated in such an
atmosphere and experience such relationships are much more likely to develop
into emotionally satisfied and balanced individuals who, as adults, will have the
motivation and the capability to act cooperatively for the good of others.

Whatever kind of classroom structure is used, the teacher will have to be
on the lookout constantly for children who seem to be isolates and gently help
them to integrate with other children. Very careful strategies must be worked
out for this purpose. Too great pushing or inculcating the feeling on the part of
the others that it is a duty to accept the loner may result in greater maladjustment
for the isolate.

In helping children to learn social skills, the teacher can select from a
varied repertoire of techniques, such as pairing children, arranging activities

for small groups, giving judicious praise or assistance, arousing interest in group activities, or utilizing the child's needs to nurture and be nurtured, to be a leader, or to follow. Methods that help a child to become comfortable and effective with other children will be detailed in Part II of this book.

EDUCATION FOR DEVELOPMENT OF MATURITY

Helping a young person to become a truly mature adult has always been an educational goal, but today the concept of maturity has had to be extended. Psychoanalysts previously defined maturity as the ability to postpone pleasure. The vast technological innovations in this century, which have brought about so much change in so short a time, have been both a blessing and a curse. They have made us aware that our resources are not limitless and that it is now necessary to consider far places and future generations in our actions. To achieve true maturity in the 1970s, it is no longer a matter of postponing certain pleasures but of giving them up altogether for the sake of others distant in time and space as well as for our contemporaries. This does not really involve great sacrifice for the individual. It means only that a giving attitude toward life needs to be substituted for the acquisitive attitude that so often predominates. The history of mankind attests that the pleasures derived from the giving attitude —enjoyment of life, creative exploration, sharing, companionship, and love—are deeply satisfying and give ultimate meaning to life.

Maturity develops by degrees. The young child is unable to imagine how even the physical world appears from a point of view different from his own at the moment. For instance, Piaget [11] found that young children, after exploring a three-dimensional landscape model, could not draw the landscape as it would appear from the side opposite to that from which they were currently viewing it. This inability to "decenter" (in Piaget's terminology) is also evident in the young child's morality. The preschool child, for example, does not judge acts as good or bad according to the intentions or situations of the people performing them but only according to whether they are punished or rewarded.

Group participation permits the child direct experience in taking alternative views. In the school environment, for example, he or she learns to perceive the school situation from the point of view of teachers and classmates and to evaluate his or her own actions from the reactions of teachers and classmates. Without this ability to "decenter," a person has only a very limited view of the consequences of his own actions. The adult who remains in the egocentric state will act like a child who plays with matches and lights a fire, unconcerned for the safety of himself and others.

Maturity not only develops by degrees, it also remains a matter of degree. Many people do not reach complete maturity. They do not learn to assume another's point of view nor to foresee the results of their own or another person's actions if their own well-being is not affected. Social immaturity often leads to personal gain; unfortunately it may lead ultimately to the destruction of the society.

EDUCATION FOR TRANSMISSION OF ETHICAL AND MORAL VALUES

Human beings can interact constructively with each other only if they share common ethical and moral values. If education is to help mankind survive, then it must take as its foremost goal the transmission of viable values. Educators must examine carefully the moral and ethical implications of all aspects of the classroom environment, including materials, methods, and physical surroundings. A sense of equality, of fairness, requires the ability to make comparisons and form judgments, taking many complex factors into account. A capacity for altruism means taking action on the basis of those judgments on behalf of others. This requires an active capacity for caring about others. Thus the development of maturity can be said to sum up all the other goals of education already enumerated, for it involves taking into account (1) survival needs, (2) skill and knowledge, (3) creative thinking, and (4) interpersonal relationships.

A fully mature person is a person who has achieved autonomous morality, the highest manifestation of which, according to Piaget, is the joining of a sense of equality with the capacity for altruism.

Teaching moral values can be attempted through the use of programed or highly structured teaching methods and/or materials, but the values emphasized in such teaching do not always reflect those needed for today's world. An analysis of one textbook series, for instance, shows that the values it conveys include such a mixed bag as affection, respect, well-being, wealth, and power—thus values that have often proved to be either disruptive or unobtainable are mixed with those necessary for survival. Books can be valuable guides in teaching, but they need to be chosen carefully. The picture on the title page of one of the books given to this writer for review shows a very angry-looking and ashamed girl, another child who seems to be laughing at her, and a third child pointing to the first. This is hardly a way to teach children love and respect. In contrast, to give one example, *The Social Sciences: Concepts and Values* [12] contains much excellent material and many valuable suggestions for helping children form viable value judgments.

In any case, values are taught most effectively not from textbooks, but by the teacher's own modeling, management, and discussion and the consequent quality of the children's own experience.

Moral and ethical values cannot be learned by the children unless they are practiced in the school. The school has to provide a classroom organization that furthers the growth and happiness of all children. It has to make provisions to assist each child to develop optimally, including children who cannot progress at the expected speed; these children can be helped by careful assessment of the causes and nature of their difficulties and the provision of an appropriate, individualized program. The school must also develop an optimum curriculum that makes the child aware of social problems, guides him to think about possible solutions, and helps him through teaching art, language arts, crafts, movement, and music to gain joy in beauty and achieve a sense of self-fulfillment.

REFERENCES

1. Neal LF, in McLean D (ed): It's People That Matter. Sydney, Austral, Angus and Robertson, 1969, p 27
2. Skinner BF: Beyond Freedom and Dignity. New York, Knopf, 1971
3. Harlow HF: Motivation as a factor in the acquisition of new responses, in Current Theory and Research in Motivation. Lincoln, University of Nebraska Press, 1953, pp 24–29
4. Goodall J vanL: The behavior of free living chimpanzees in the Gombe stream reserve. Anim Behav Monographs 1(3):161–311, 1968
5. Hinde RA: Some problems in the study of the development of social behavior, in Tobach E, Aronson LR, Shaw E (eds): The Biopsychology of Development. New York, Academic Press, 1971
6. Piaget J: Biology and Knowledge. Chicago, University of Chicago Press, 1971
7. Koestler A: The Act of Creation. New York, Macmillan, 1964
8. Koestler A: Ghost in the Machine. New York, Macmillan, 1968
9. Copland A: Music and imagination (Charles Eliot Norton lectures, 1951–1952), reported in Storr A: The Dynamics of Creation. New York, Atheneum, 1972
10. Harlow HF, Harlow MK: The affectional systems, in Schrier AM, Harlow HF, Stollnitz F (eds): Behavior of Nonhuman Primates, vol. 2. New York, Academic Press, 1965, pp 287–334
11. Piaget J, Inhelder B: The Child's Conception of Space. London, Routledge and Kegan Paul, 1956
12. Brandwein PF, et al: Social Sciences: Concepts and Values. New York, Harcourt Brace Jovanovich, 1970

2
The Problems of Education in Our Time

> *There is an immense task incumbent on all men of good will, namely, the task of restoring the relations of the human family in truth, in justice, in love, and in freedom.*
>
> *Pope John XXIII* [1, p 155]

As we have discussed, the major goals of present-day education can be classified under six headings:

1. Survival, comfort, and security of the individual, of his group, and of all humanity
2. Satisfaction of the need for skills and knowledge
3. Satisfaction of the needs for exploration, creativity, and self-realization
4. Satisfaction of the needs for human relationships
5. Development of maturity
6. Transmission of ethical and moral values

Educators today often seem unaware of these goals; they frequently do not even aspire to them; only a small number of schools are committed to working for their realization. But survival itself is at stake. Children must be equipped to understand and deal with problems of land depletion and erosion, water shortages and pollution, seed and food storage and distribution, and overpopulation. They must learn the consequences of the hydrogen bomb if they are to defend themselves—from themselves.

The economic and technological revolutions have lifted the goals of education from a local to a worldwide perspective. To meet this challenge, educational institutions must ask themselves whether they teach static facts or dynamic relationships; do they teach what is known rather than ways of tackling new problems; do they perpetuate division rather than foster cooperation and understanding among groups; and do they neglect to nurture love of beauty and the need for discovery?

The goals of education are not easily achieved. Our world is neither secure nor comfortable; for many children even survival itself is impossible. Under such circumstances the needs for knowledge, creativity, and self-realization fade into the background and the need for interpersonal relationships becomes subservient to the need for survival.

When a culture is destroyed because of the continuous threat to life, transmission of the culture becomes impossible. Nevertheless, whenever living conditions permit an existence only slightly above the survival level, the school clings to its age-old task of transmitting the skills regarded as essential to any civilization. In adverse circumstances, however, the learning of these skills may become a heavy burden for the child.

As a result, many children in the developing nations of the world, for example, cannot advance beyond the first or second grade, either because they are overworked and undernourished, or because the traditional curriculum is meaningless for them, or because they lack the clothes, books, and materials needed in school.

Even in the more developed countries many children lack the preconditions for healthy development and therefore for optimum learning. Smooth development in childhood generally seems to depend on the availability of stable conditions, which are often lacking even in affluent societies. The security of children at any social level can be threatened by divorce of the parents, severe family discord, and changes in location that require giving up established patterns. Many children are required to make adjustments to a new location, a new culture, and a new language simultaneously. In one public school classroom in which the author worked, only 5 of 40 children had not experienced one or more severe disruptions in their lives; it was no wonder that the children's ability to learn and to adjust was adversely affected. The situation in this classroom was not atypical.

In poor districts the world over children frequently experience the teacher as a stranger who has nothing in common with them. This was expressed poignantly by a 13-year-old girl who said to a substitute teacher, "When the bell rings, the teachers drive away in their cars. They do not know about us and how we live."

THE NUTURING ROLE OF THE SCHOOL

One of the major problems with which modern education is confronted is the necessity for integrating effectively into the classrooms broad groups of very different children. Many children who live in conditions of poverty and many children who are attempting to cope with a new environment do not progress well in school. These children may be lagging in essential abilities, such as language skills, or their inner conflicts may leave them with too little energy or with too much anger to enable them to learn or to adjust. In addition, an increasing number of children are reported to be handicapped by neurological dysfunctions that affect their ability to benefit from the school experience. Others have physical defects. There are also children who are unusually highly gifted and able to progress at a faster pace than their classmates. All of these children need an adjustment of the school program.

Many children are caught up in a self-fulfilling prophecy. The conditions under which they live are likely to induce feelings of lack of control over their own lives and the expectation that their future will be insecure, poverty-bound, and meaningless. They see older relatives and high school and even college

Fig. 2-1. This young volunteer finds helping children a most rewarding and self-fulfilling experience. His students share his enthusiasm. (Photo by James Quinn and Michael Campa.)

graduates among them out of work.* Their negative or apathetic attitude toward school, combined with experienced discrepancy between home culture and school, leads to many of them becoming "dropouts." A dropout is often considered unemployable because employers assume him to be hostile, unsocialized, and unreliable. And thus negative expectations are fulfilled. Many turn to violence as a release for their frustrations or to drug addiction as an escape from their surroundings.

Schools are indeed overwhelmed by the task of educating the economically disadvantaged, the socially different, the children who speak another language, or the children who lack positive experiences. Many children feel like strangers in their schools; at home they may also feel very much alone because their parents, too, feel strange and insecure and overwhelmed. Many schools give up and passively accept the fact that some children, even entire groups of children, fall farther and farther behind their more privileged agemates.

Educators more than ever before must take into account the affective life of all children as well as their cognitive functions in planning the school curriculum and creating a school atmosphere conducive for all to learn. All children, not only those with special educational needs, can only develop optimally in a school atmosphere that is warm, caring, and responsive. *Education must exercise a nurturing as well as a teaching role.*

UNIFORMITY OF TEACHING

A visitor to school classrooms in most countries is likely to find all children being taught the same things in the same way. Such uniformity may be considered necessary because of economic considerations, as in most developing countries, or because it is mandated by departments or boards of education, or because it is still felt that education consists of filling children's heads with a "divinely revealed" body of knowledge to be taught in traditionally prescribed ways. But the imposition of such educational conformity harms not only the less able child, who may give up and view himself as an utter failure, but also the gifted child, who may become bored and disruptive. As Donald Anderson of Australia remarked in reference to education in his country, "Education has become so equal that it is anaemic" [3].

The poor results of a uniform education have been observed by the author. For example, a number of children have been referred to our center† from

---

*The 1975 national unemployment rate for young men between the ages of 16 and 21 was 19.2 percent. The 1975 national unemployment rate for young urban black men was 31.9 percent [2].

†The Marianne Frostig Center of Educational Therapy in Los Angeles.

schools located in the United States and Europe who had been unable to learn and were considered behavior problems. However, we found the children to be both intelligent and highly sensitive. They had been shamed several times in front of their former classmates because they had not attended to the class assignments, and they had been excluded from games because they had coordination or other slight disabilities. Thus, they withdrew from the school situation. A few were gifted children who had shown their boredom in school. With proper support and individualized attention, these children regained their self-confidence and were able to return to regular school and proceed successfully after a relatively short period of remediation.

Providing equality of opportunity in education should not be confused with providing identical education. As Anderson concludes, "Equality of opportunity can be defined, not only to include equal exposure for all, but the opportunity to overcome obstacles to the development of ability" [3]. Democratic education requires that every child should receive the kind of education that is optimum for him. As children differ, optimum education will differ in consequence.

THE EDUCATION EXPLOSION

Neither the nurturing nor the teaching roles can be exercised if the child is not regarded as being a member of a community as well as an individual. Education is always influenced by the culture and by the totality of living conditions. A particular need or group of needs may be of critical educational concern because of the socioeconomic condition of a country or region at a given point in time. For example, illiteracy and hunger are problems experienced today in most of the Third World, and malnutrition and unemployment threaten the majority of countries. In these nations, the emphasis in education is the mastery of the basic skills. In the industrialized nations, on the other hand, most educational institutions emphasize preparation for the more sophisticated job market and the achievement of better relations among cultural and ethnic groups. The immediate educational needs of the community, therefore, have to be satisfied.

While the goals of education become increasingly difficult to achieve for increasingly large numbers of children in our strife-torn and overpopulated world, paradoxically the literacy rate, even in the poorest countries, is rising. Countries pride themselves on the number of children enrolled in school and the children are expected by their parents and by the civil authorities to attend and to achieve.

In fact, the most conspicuous trend in education during this last century has been the institution of compulsory universal education. In the Soviet

Union, for instance, literacy has increased from 10 percent in the 1920s to over 98 percent in 1972 [4]. The trend to include more and more children within the bounds of general education is paralleled by a trend to lengthen the time of compulsory attendance. School attendance in the United States is required until children reach the age of 16. In several states, children are expected to stay in school until 18 years of age. (As a matter of fact, the number of junior colleges and other institutions of postsecondary education is large enough in many states to permit any youth who so desires to attend, for a minimal tuition fee, until the age of 20.) France has raised the age of leaving school from 14 to 16. In England school-based education for all children has been extended to age 16 as a consequence of the publication of a report by the Central Advisory Council for Education, *Half of Our Future* [5].

When lack of money is necessitating curtailment of educational services, even in the relatively affluent countries, and overpopulation is making it difficult to provide needed services in countries with a huge birth rate or massive immigration, why is this trend so conspicuous? One reason is that technological advances require higher educational levels. Another is that current economic conditions, with massive unemployment, suggest keeping children in school longer; there will be less competition in the restricted job market, and also compulsory attendance will keep the youths off the street and out of trouble.

The gradual broadening of exposure to education, not only in schools but also by means of the worldwide increase in facilities for travel and communication, has itself created a demand for more education. There seems to be a global hunger for knowledge. These trends, though admirable, present education with further problems.

How have the schools reacted to the challenge of increased and prolonged school attendance? They have reacted not by changing but simply by reproducing. More and more schools have been built, but the teaching recapitulates old models designed to meet old goals, and the curriculum for the most part has not been made relevant to the world in which today's children find themselves. The least change has taken place at the secondary level, which is also the place of greatest student unrest.

In the traditional high school students see teachers as having knowledge, not necessarily related in any way to the students' circumstances and interest, that they impart whole in a building especially consecrated to that purpose. The "real life" learning and teaching that these students experience in a great variety of ways and places, and usually related to their immediate needs and interests, have no place in the school curricula nor is their existence even acknowledged by the teaching staff. Schooling, therefore, becomes for many an unreal ritual quite irrelevant to their needs and experience.

Not only have the secondary schools generally been unresponsive to changing social conditions, but they have also continued to act as social class agents. Secondary schools and colleges hold the key to job success and upward mobility. Their procedures of testing, tracking, "guidance" counseling, and so on effectively circumscribe the socioeconomic niche of the student. The procedures, which reflect the current status quo, may be considered necessary and helpful by well-meaning educators; but, as S. M. Miller and P. A. Roby point out, they tend to put students into slots [6]. It is not surprising that there is anger and unrest.

REFERENCES

1. Pope John XXIII: Peace on Earth. New York, Ridge Press/Odyssey Press, 1964
2. U.S. Department of Labor. Employment and Earnings 22:139, 1976
3. Anderson D: Equality of education, in McLean D (ed): It's People That Matter. Sydney, Austral, Angus and Robertson, 1969
4. Caldwell B: Lecture presented at the Neuropsychiatric Institute, University of California, Los Angeles, July 16, 1973
5. Newson J (chmn): Half of Our Future, a report of the Central Advisory Council for Education. London, Her Majesty's Stationery Office, 1963
6. Miller SM, Roby PA: Social mobility, equality, and education, in Havighurst RJ et al (eds): Society and Education: A Book of Readings. Boston, Allyn and Bacon, 1971

3
The Problem of the Child with Special Instructional Needs

Education shall be directed to the full development of the human personality and to the strengthening of respect for human rights and fundamental freedoms.

Universal Declaration of Human Rights
[1, Article 26, Paragraph 2]

Knowledge and skills are not easily acquired by all children. Large groups of children who pose special problems must also be served adequately by the school system. Among these groups is one frequently labeled "children with special learning disabilities." Increasingly, convention programs for educators and psychologists, lay and professional publications, television programs, and meetings of particular parent groups have been devoted to analyzing, discussing, and suggesting remedies for the plight of these children.

The most common American definition of the child with special learning disabilities is that suggested by the National Advisory Committee on Handicapped Children in 1968. This definition has been used in state and federal educational legislation:

Children with special learning disabilities exhibit a disorder in one or more of the basic psychological processes involved in understanding or in using spoken or written languages. These may be manifested in disorders of listening, thinking, talking, reading, writing, spelling, or arithmetic. They include conditions which have been referred to as perceptual handicaps, brain injury, minimal brain dysfunction, dyslexia, developmental aphasia, etc. They do not include learning problems which are due primarily to visual, hearing, or motor handicaps, to mental retardation, to emotional disturbance, or to environmental disadvantage. [2, p 73]

In this book we will not be restricted to studying only this ill-defined group of children. Currently, educable mentally retarded children and emotionally disturbed children, as well as children with special learning disabilities, are more and more frequently educated in the same classroom as the so-called normal child. For the classroom teacher, distinctions between groups of children who need her special attention become blurred. Besides, the causation in most children with learning problems is multiple. Emotional disturbance, severe economic deprivation, and deficits in communication and cognition tend to occur together. We will, therefore, include all children with learning problems in our discussion and refer to them as "children with special instructional needs." This designation has the additional advantage of eradicating much of the stigma of labels, such as retarded, emotionally disturbed, or minimally brain damaged.

Children with special instructional needs comprise a sizable part of the school population of all countries with compulsory school attendance, ranging from less than 10 percent in some areas to 60 percent or 80 percent in certain schools. For example, Marlene Sheppard, Inspector of Education, New South Wales, stated that in certain Australian schools with a predominantly migrant population about 60 percent to 80 percent of the children need adjustments in the curriculum and teaching methods to be able to progress satisfactorily in school [3].

In the United States two contrasting points of view underlie the measures currently used for helping children with special instructional needs. One approach is to provide special tutoring and remedial procedures for short daily periods while allowing the children to remain in their regular classroom. The other approach is based on a medical model, with classificatory diagnosis followed by segregation into special classrooms or schools, such as those for the learning disabled, the mentally retarded, the emotionally disturbed, or the educationally handicapped. Until recently the second approach has been the usual procedure, but there is now a welcome movement in many school districts to integrate children with special instructional needs into the regular classes. Even those children who are assigned to a special classroom are often permitted to attend a regular classroom for part of the day.*

---

*The Council of Exceptional Children has explicitly favored such a policy in its statement in the journal *Exceptional Children* [4]. In the same issue also see articles by L. C. Burrello and others [5] and by F. Warner and others [6].

THE LOS ANGELES MODEL

The model developed for children with special instructional needs by the Department of Special Education in Los Angeles permits an unusual degree of flexibility in integrating these children into the school population and providing for their educational needs. The program was introduced gradually in the early seventies. Its effectiveness is dependent on the training of the teachers employed, the continuing amount of available money, and the degree of cooperation of a large and diversified staff. Here we shall only be concerned with the design of the program, which most certainly merits discussion.

Ernest Willenberg, Assistant Superintendent of the Division of Special Education, Los Angeles City Schools, addressing the International Rehabilitation Medicine Association, in October 1974 discussed what he called the pyramid of educational services for all handicapped children, the majority of whom are the economically underprivileged and the learning handicapped [7]. The Los Angeles model follows his pyramid. The first step of the pyramid is comprised of adjunctive services, such as transportation and medical treatment. The second step is supplemental teaching in the regular classroom; the teacher is trained to assist children with special instructional needs within the classroom, often with the assistance of an aide. The third step is specialized supplementary teaching of the handicapped child outside the regular classroom; this is often done by a resource room teacher for a limited number of hours per week. Day class instruction is the fourth step; the handicapped child receives most instruction in a special classroom within the school but is integrated with agemates whenever possible. At the fifth step the handicapped child receives instruction in a special school. Home and hospital teaching constitutes the sixth step, and at the seventh step the child is maximally segregated from society, as is the case for those confined to correctional institutions.

Willenberg noted that there were approximately 60,000 handicapped children in Los Angeles, of whom as of 1974 only half were receiving services on any step of the pyramid. He did point out that when adequate services were not available, the child could be referred to a private agency.

For the teacher with a child who has special instructional needs, Willenberg has grouped into four major areas the steps that should be taken to help the child [8]:

1. *Remediating underlying handicaps.* Special methods of helping the child develop his basic psychological functions have to be selected and used, especially when the child lags behind his agemates. Functional diagnosis (as opposed to etiological diagnosis) is therefore extremely important. Sensory-motor functions, perceptual skills, language, higher thought processes (such as memory, classifying, seriation, problem solving), and

social and emotional development all have to be evaluated. School psychologists, paramedical personnel, physicians, or multidisciplinary clinical teams may assist in the evaluation, but the teacher is the pivotal figure in any appraisal of the child's ability to function in school. In many, if not most, educational settings the entire educational evaluation of the child is the responsibility of the teacher. And it is always the responsibility of the teacher, on the basis of the evaluation, to choose and adapt materials and methods to help each child enhance and develop optimally his basic learning skills.

2. *Helping the child to adjust behaviorally.* Appropriate classroom behavior has to be taught. This includes such behavior as orientation to a task, sustained attention to a task, and avoidance of disturbing behavior (destructiveness, unnecessary noise, teasing, or fighting). The child also has to learn to be self-directive and orderly. It is necessary to know where to keep books, where to get an eraser, how to pour juice, when to help another child, where to put materials that are not in use, when to empty the trash basket, how to greet visitors, and so on.

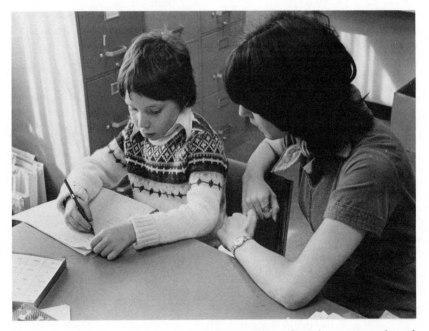

Fig. 3-1. Special manuscript exercises help a child to form letters correctly and organize and plan his paper. Special methods of teaching need to be devised for children with special instructional needs. (Photo by James Quinn and Michael Campa.)

3. *Devising specific methods of teaching.* The teacher must devise methods for the child with special needs so that child will be able to make progress academically, even when his specific deficits have not been ameliorated. The teacher has to help all children to experience success and to enjoy school.
4. *Helping the child to develop socially and emotionally.* This last task will often involve establishing optimum relationships between the family and the child, between the child and peers, and even between the child and the family's cultural group. This broad task, consequently, will include work with the whole community.
5. The author proposes adding to these four tasks a fifth one—*assisting the child in understanding ethical considerations.* What are a person's responsibilities with regard to others? What is the meaning of being human—or what should it be?

SOME EDUCATIONAL PRINCIPLES FOR CHILDREN WITH SPECIAL INSTRUCTIONAL NEEDS

After careful research Sylvia Farnham-Diggory [9] has concluded that a preschool program *integrating sensorimotor, perceptual, and language training* will help the majority of children from disadvantaged backgrounds. This approach has also been found optimal for children who suffer from learning deficits or who are emotionally disturbed. Essentially the same strategy applies to all, because all of these children are characterized by a lag in developmental abilities.

In addition, the teacher must *choose the specific teaching techniques and emphasize the specific areas that are appropriate for each child's individual pattern of abilities and disabilities.* An initial assessment of the child's total characteristics and his abilities and disabilities in all major developmental skills is necessary for optimum teaching.

Finally, the teacher must be aware that for a child to make good use of an experience, *the experience must have significance for him.* Significance, in turn, depends on previous experiences: it is the relationship between what the child already knows and the present experience that is a precondition for significant learning. Any child who lacks the necessary fund of experiences, for whatever reason, cannot learn from the regular school curriculum and will fall further and further behind agemates.

Thus, individualized training programs are necessary for the child who has difficulties in progressing in school, whether the cause is considered to be learning disabilities or socioeconomic disadvantage or emotional disturbance. Such programs must include sensorimotor, perceptual, and language training as well as a rich variety of experiences and be in accord with the child's past experiences.

LABELING AND SEGREGATION

Labeling and segregation for educational purposes of children with learning difficulties from children with emotional disturbances or from those who are environmentally disadvantaged should be discouraged. The reasons are manifold.

The socioeconomically disadvantaged child as well as the child with learning disabilities may fail in the regular classroom because he lags or is inadequate in abilities necessary for school learning. The research of B. Pasamanick and his associates [10] has shown that a large percentage of economically deprived children suffer from specific learning disabilities. Maternal malnutrition, difficult or prolonged birth, inadequate infant feeding, a high incidence of injury and disease combined with lack of medical care—all such factors are known to affect the developing central nervous system. Lack of relevant experiences combined with a possibility of neurological impairment combine to make the socioeconomically disadvantaged child a high educational risk if appropriate educational procedures and nutrition and health services are not available for the child.

For the educator the end result is the same as for children with learning disabilities who are not socioeconomically deprived. An analysis of the essential psychological abilities (sensorimotor abilities, perception, language, and thought processes) reveals that deficits in these skills characterize both groups. Many children in these groups also suffer from emotional disturbances. Usually causation and symptoms are mixed, but the lack of necessary and rewarding experiences is a common causative factor. The socioeconomically disadvantaged child often cannot function in school because his environment has not offered him these experiences; the learning deficient child cannot function because his cognitive and communicative deviations have made it difficult or impossible for him to make use of them; the emotionally disturbed child cannot respond to the outside world because he is preoccupied with his problems. Thus, it is usually unnecessary or even impossible to separate these groups for educational purposes. All of these children need individualized teaching methods and training in basic skills if they are to make academic progress, regardless of etiology.

Moreover, classificatory approaches often lead to the neglect of those symptoms that do not fit the category. For instance, emotional disturbance, which is nearly universal in children with neurological symptoms, may not be taken into account in educational programing for children assigned to a class for the "neurologically handicapped." In the same way cognitive disabilities of children may be overlooked in a class designated "emotionally disturbed." Any treatment program must take into account *every* aspect of every child's development.

Labeling children is also to be discouraged because it causes unnecessary feelings of abnormality and separateness and, therefore, may lead to anxiety and to loss of self-esteem among children and parents [11]. It also has the insidious effect, sometimes unconsciously, of causing teachers to lower their expectations of labeled children [12] so that the teachers themselves contribute to the failure they anticipate and the label becomes a self-fulfilling prophecy.

For all of these reasons we choose to favor the term *children with special educational needs,* a group that includes gifted children as well as those described above. It is vitally important to note, also, that for all of these reasons *testing and evaluation of children should not be undertaken merely for purposes of categorizing them—but in order to provide the teacher with comprehensive and specific knowledge of a child's abilities and disabilities so that an optimum education program can be established.*

PROGRAMS FOR CHILDREN WITH SPECIAL INSTRUCTIONAL NEEDS

Preventive Measures

An increasing emphasis is now being placed on trying to prevent, as well as to remedy, learning and adjustment difficulties. Head Start, for example, is an innovative program designed to prepare economically disadvantaged preschool children in the United States for attendance in regular kindergarten and primary school classes. The Follow-Through projects extend Head Start through the primary grades and in some school districts through elementary (junior) school, supplementing the regular school program in ways that vary from district to district. Such programs are designed not only to help prevent learning difficulties but also to help the child feel comfortable in school and to contribute to his security.

New Programs

The most striking characteristic of the newly emerging programs in general education is their diversity, even where the purpose is uniform (as in Head Start or Follow-Through programs). The basic philosophy may vary from an emphasis on self-direction to a conditioning (behavioristic) approach and from regarding the function of the school as serving the whole community to regarding it only as providing an academic education for children. Even in the more traditional schools a broadening of the curricula is occurring and the interests of the children are increasingly taken into account. The desire of the school personnel to have the cooperation of the community leads to greater effort in seeking contact with the parents, and this practice leads to better understanding of the experiences and needs of the children. These trends in educational attitudes seem on the way to becoming established practices. They point to a significant goal of the future—to establish a variety of programs that enable individual differences in interests and experience to be taken into account. The terms *individualization* and even *personalization* (giving personal meaning to what is taught) are seen and heard with increasing frequency in education circles—and even in the community at large. This trend undoubtedly will intensify in the school environment as new ways of individualizing and personalizing teaching are developed. It will be expressed both through the institution of new programs and by the adoption of more flexible methods of classroom management.

The common characteristic underlying all new forms of education is that they are planned to serve the needs of individual children and their families instead of requiring children to fit the mold designed by the schools. That educators recognize this goal is evidenced by such measures as the adjustment of curricula to the needs and abilities of the handicapped child and the institution of innovative projects characterized by diversified and individualized curricula, designed to satisfy the interest of the children. Several of these programs will be discussed in the next chapter.

The importance of helping children to find satisfaction in human relationships is also considered. Most of today's innovative classrooms regard this as important an educational goal as acquiring academic expertise. Helping the child to enjoy interpersonal relationships with classmates and teachers not only makes life in school more pleasant, it also lays the groundwork for the child's present and future mental health. It develops the capacity to appreciate the feelings and values of others and prepares the child for cooperative effort in all aspects of his life.

Forces Impeding Change

Nevertheless, strong forces still delay the necessary changes in education in many countries. Teaching and parenthood suffer from what has been called a cultural lag. Childhood experiences are powerful shapers of later life, and our memories concerning our parents, teachers, and schools make it difficult for us to envision quite different kinds of relationships and procedures with regard to our own children. The model of the parent or teacher of the past always intrudes. Practitioners of medicine, law, and other professions are fortunate by comparison: they were not exposed to professional models when they were impressionably young!

The morals, customs, and institutions of the past were forms of adaptation to past circumstances. The morals, customs, and institutions of the present and future must be appropriate for a different and swiftly changing environment. And it is education that provides the means to meet this challenge. Teacher training, however, has been slow to adapt to new requirements. As Arnold S. Toynbee, the historian, has pointed out, a new era requires adaptation or the culture dies.

It is still but a hope that schools will teach all children that the future of mankind depends on the actions of men today, that the globe has become too small to exclude any country or any race from present considerations, that technological changes have to be applied with caution, that the earth will only nourish our souls and bodies when we do not abuse her. At present we still have to be satisfied, on the whole, with more limited attempts at change. Some practical examples of steps for change will be given in the next chapter.

REFERENCES

1. United Nations General Assembly: Universal Declaration of Human Rights, adopted December 10, 1948
2. National Advisory Committee on Handicapped Children: Special Education for Handicapped Children. Washington, DC, US Office of Education, 1968
3. Sheppard M: Personal communication, 1973
4. Council of Exceptional Children. Policy statement. Exceptional Children 40(1):70–73, 1973
5. Burrello LC, Tracy M, Schultz E: Special education as experimental education; A new conceptualization. Exceptional Children 40(1):29–34, 1973
6. Warner F, et al: Attitudes of children toward their special class placement. Exceptional Children 40(1):37–38, 1973
7. Willenberg EP: Special education and rehabilitation. Paper presented at the Second Congress of the International Rehabilitation Medicine Association, Mexico City, October 1974
8. Willenberg EP: Methods and techniques of psychopedagogic treatment. Paper presented at the Second Congress of the International Rehabilitation Medicine Association, Mexico City, October 1974
9. Farnham-Diggory S: Cognitive synthesis in Negro and white children. Monographs of the Society for Research in Child Development 35(135), 1970
10. Pasamanick B, et al: Socioeconomic status and some precursors of neurosychiatric disorders. Am J Orthopsychiatry 26:594–601, 1956
11. Edgerton RB, Edgerton CR: Becoming mentally retarded in an Hawaiian school, in Tarjan G, Eyman R, Meyers CE (eds): Sociobehavioral Studies in Mental

Retardation: Papers in Honor of Harvey F. Dingman. Monographs of the American Association on Mental Deficiency (1), 1973

12. Rosenthal R, Jacobson L: Pygmalion in the Classroom: Teacher Expectation and Pupils' Intellectual Development. New York, Holt, 1968

PART II

Promoting Behavioral Changes through the Classroom Structure

Introduction

To the injunction, "Teach your pupil to think," I should like to add a further injunction, "Teach your pupil to see and feel."
Sir Richard Livingstone [1, p 102]

If education is to reach the goals that we have discussed and be a force for positive change in the world, it is imperative to consider what changes must be made within the educational structure. Certain traditional practices clearly need to be amended. We cannot help children to become responsible if we do not permit them to take responsibility. We cannot help children learn to cooperate if they sit in five straight rows, facing front, not permitted to speak. We cannot help children to care for each other if we track them into ever more homogeneous groups. We cannot help children to plan if all plans are made by the teacher. We cannot help children to find their own best ways of learning if all are required to learn in the same way. We cannot help children to become deeply involved in learning, doing, and creating if we continually interrupt them with bells and schedules. If we are unable to make the necessary accommodations to help children, we are working against the interests both of children and of society.

Somehow we have to find forms that will provide greater flexibility and diversity for both students and teachers. If teachers are not permitted to alter their classroom structures, at least to some degree, they will have difficulty in attempting to meet education's goals. Change in structure is necessary if education is to affect

. . . the progress and the well-being not only of the class as a whole, but

37

also of each child within it. This requires, on the teacher's part, an organization which specifically caters to the individual multiplied by every child in the class. And on the child's part, the requirement is that he, the individual, can recognize and comprehend the organization, can conduct himself within it so that his need for activity and participation is met, and yet can share the attention and the resources of his teacher with many others whose needs are similar to his own [2, p 15].

In Chapter 4 we shall look briefly at some aspects of education that have on the whole been given little attention. If moves toward alternatives in education are to be successful, these need to be carefully considered. Whereas methods, books, and workshops proliferate and curricula emerge faster than one can pick up publishers' brochures, teachers working in the real world often find little to help them when they deal with such problems as complementing the experiences of children at home and in the community, counseling children, and promoting parent and community relations. Administrators, too, when attempting to evaluate new programs or trying to find ways of helping teachers prepare themselves for positive change, often find themselves equally alone. Chapter 4 offers some suggestions in these areas.

Chapter 5 is devoted to a more detailed discussion of a variety of alternative approaches in education. In particular, there is an extended account of an open-classroom program in Hartford, Connecticut. This is followed by a detailed description of a more restricted project in Compton, California, designed to expand an existing program of early education in a disadvantaged community by introducing ability training into that program.

REFERENCES

1. Livingston R: Education and the Spirit of the Age. Oxford, Carendon Press, 1952
2. Taylor J: Organizing the Open Classroom. New York, Shocken, 1972

4

The Nurturing Role of the School

The life of the whole institution was like that of one happy family, the strongest attachment existed between all the members of it and one enjoyed at the same time the rarest and purest pleasures, which acquaintance with nature and art can afford.

Ramsauer, speaking of Pestalozzi's school [1, p 38]

After the age of 5 or 6 (and sometimes even earlier) children spend a great part of their lives in school. The quality of school life—what might be called its "psychological ecology"—necessarily strongly influences the entire subsequent course of a child's growing up.

Many children today are deprived and anxiety-ridden. Many live in the restrictive environments of big cities. Other children live in areas torn by war or racial strife or lacking in rule of law. Some live in dire socioeconomic circumstances, with little shelter and no assurance that they will have food the next day. Migrant children may live with the anxiety of coping with an alien environment and language, while their parents may themselves feel displaced and threatened by loss of jobs.

Not only inner-city and socioeconomically disadvantaged children live in conditions that do not satisfy their needs. Any environment may furnish forms of stress or deprivation which adversely affect a child's development. For instance, the well-to-do child in the United States can be disadvantaged because he is cared for by a maid who comes from a foreign rural environment, speaks little English, and has little in common with the child. He may, therefore, suffer from loneliness and lack of communication. A middle-class child in a traditional school, be it in the United States, Europe, Australia, or

South America, may be chronically anxious because he knows that his parents will feel disappointed if he does not pass the next exam, with honors. Some older middle-class children may be in conflict with their families because they disagree with their parents' values, social aspirations, or mechanical adherence to the status quo. Sometimes children are ill treated by their parents. Everywhere they are affected by the prevalence of crumbling family structures and fears of the loss of love. Studies show that television viewing can contribute its share of fear, anxiety, and confusion also [2].

To educate healthy and happy children, *the school must complement, and in some instances provide restitution for, the home and the social milieu*. All schools must assume responsibility for nurturing children.

This chapter will focus on five aspects which reflect the nurturing role of the school: classroom organization, physical environment, meeting the needs of individual children, counseling, and the community–school relationship.

CLASSROOM ORGANIZATION

The school environment is never quite natural. It is not natural for a child to spend many hours daily with so many other children and a single adult. It is unnatural to sit in the classroom when the playground beckons outside. It is unnatural to stand in line quietly while 30 or more children are assembled.

Generally, nursery schools and kindergartens do not impose vigorous discipline or confront children with academic learning, and youngsters at this level generally appear to be alert, happy, and eager. Even at these levels, though, school conditions can gradually become more restrictive and demanding. In kindergarten or first grade, children are often required to sit quietly at their desks and are not permitted to talk except when asked a question. In many cases contact with peers is permitted only briefly and infrequently. The activities are usually teacher-chosen, teacher-directed, and teacher-regulated. These are all exceedingly taxing conditions for a young child, and the effort to adapt to them may prove overwhelming, absorbing most of the child's energies and leaving little for learning.

A rigid impersonal school situation is difficult even for those children whose home environments provide them with security and freedom to move, to communicate with others, and to explore the world around them. Unfortunately these natural rights of childhood are grossly curtailed for hundreds of thousands of children, regardless of socioeconomic level, and the school, which should afford them the opportunity to enjoy these rights, instead restricts them further. When very young, children tend to respond with passivity; they submit to the regime, for they have no other choice. As they grow older, they may show increasing anxiety, an active dislike of school, and possibly rebellion.

Undesirable and destructive results can only be avoided if the school nurtures the children in its care; that is, if it attempts to meet their genuine needs for self-initiated activities and for communication.

PHYSICAL ENVIRONMENT

The urban landscape that confronts too many children can only be described as dreary and ugly. Today with the continuous spread of urban slums it is an even greater disadvantage than it was in earlier times for the school environment to be bereft of beauty and comfort.

Beauty is important not only with regard to the children's sensibilities but also with respect to their academic performance. As J. F. Mackworth points out, children in an attractive school work and read better; a dreary place makes them lose interest [3]. The classroom environment most conducive to learning can best be characterized by the adjectives "cozy" and "homey." The child becomes habituated much more quickly in such a classroom, and such an atmosphere contributes to his freedom from anxiety, which, in turn, helps him to increase his attention span and thereby enables him to learn more.

Although it is the poor child living in a drab, depressive, and unstimulating environment who needs a pleasant school environment the most, it is ironic that, in general, the poorer the children comprising a particular school's population, the poorer the equipment and the building. This is true in the United States as well as in other countries of the world. Even in well-developed communities, classrooms and school buildings are apt to be drab and poorly equipped.

If schools are to fulfill the objectives of education, they must be attractive, warm, nurturing places. Fortunately, there are teachers who can do wonders and provide a beautiful and stimulating environment with a small budget and in relatively old and dilapidated buildings.

MEETING THE NEEDS OF INDIVIDUAL CHILDREN

All classroom structures, no matter what the model, must adapt to the needs of individual children, needs that may vary at different times during the school day. At any given time, some children may need very rigid structuring, clearly defined, because their own weak ego development and great anxiety do not yet permit them to deal with the ambiguities and decision making involved in greater independence. Other children may at the same time benefit most from great freedom of movement and independent exploration.

In one corner of a classroom structured to meet individual needs might be a group of children planning a trip and its subsequent follow-up. Elsewhere two children might be working with flash cards, as prescribed in their work assignments, while in another part of the room a small group, carefully supervised and encouraged, is completing assignments clearly laid out for them in work folders.

Not only structure and, of course, teaching methods must vary but more subtle factors, such as pacing of work, emotional climate, and the provision of opportunities for various kinds of social interaction must also be adopted. For instance, there might be in the same classroom Mitch, who is always tired, listless, and discouraged and who always looks for the teacher to help him, Harold, who bristles when the teacher comes near him, and Lyle, who likes to work by herself, proceeding steadily and with enjoyment. The teacher will have to give much encouragement to Mitch, who really needs it, while Harold may do better working alone with a teaching machine or programmed workbook. Lyle's ability and capacity for concentrated effort might be used in tutoring other children so she learns to adopt a compassionate leadership role.

A very important task of the teacher is to assess such factors through observation. (A fuller discussion of this is found in Part III.) The teacher will often have to proceed by trial and error, with frequent reevaluating, but always following the general rule—discontinue what does not work and continue with what does. The teacher who continues with the same reading method although a particular child shows frustration or who forces an anxious child to play on the playground with others although tears and temper tantrums are the results fails the child. Phonics may be an important aid to learning for one child but a deterrent for others. Playing a ball game with the group may be an enjoyable and highly educational activity for most of the children, but being forced to join may cause a withdrawn child to become even more withdrawn.

Knowing when methods do not work and when approaches need change is usually very difficult. It requires especially sensitive observation or "seeing." Lillian Weber writes:

> Perhaps the important estimate the teacher must make in her "seeing" is whether a child is growing at all, whether he has stopped growing, whether in fact something is blocking growth—in which cases, there is a distinct indication to see further and indeed to seek help outside the teaching role for the "seeing" [4, p 5].

The fine art of "seeing" in this sense is given little time in most teacher-training programs. The work of J. Gellert [5] and Ira Gordon [6] will prove most helpful to the teacher in search of further specific guidance, as will two publications of the North Dakota Study Group on Alternative Evaluation [7, 8].

In every aspect of education, careful individualization is necessary to

Fig. 4-1.   A good teacher provides counseling, warm support, and needed structure.
(Photo by James Quinn and Michael Campa.)

eliminate, or at least to diminish, difficulties and to help children realize their
full potential. This author believes that a teacher who becomes committed to
any *single* narrowly defined method of classroom management or instruction
will only be able to classify children into two groups: those who have benefitted
and those who have failed.

COUNSELING

A good school will attempt to make up for at least some of the deficits and
disturbances in the child's life. All schools should be therapeutic, but this is
possible only when the teaching staff cares for the children's total well-being

and when schools genuinely regard this function as an intrinsic part of the teacher's role. Too frequently this obligation has not been officially recognized. Nevertheless, there have always been teachers who have placed it foremost in their regard.

On a visit to a one-room school for native Fijian children, the author was impressed with the general openness and happiness of the children, as well as with their industry. The teacher was occupied in consoling a little boy who was clinging like a leech to his leg. He told the author, "I am sorry, but I can't talk to you now. This child's mother is ill, and he needs my attention. Please forgive me and come back a bit later." This teacher's attitude was quite correct. The well-being of his charge was the first priority.

A teacher who takes as his or her first priority the overall well-being of each child assumes a counseling role. The teacher–child relationship is a most important one for the child, at least in elementary school. That relationship, characterized by trust and acceptance, becomes the indispensable foundation for helping the child—and often his parents too—whenever difficulties arise.

Many teachers feel uncomfortable and incompetent in the counseling role. Traditional teacher-training programs have, in general, not taught formal counseling skills, and school administrators have usually acted as if the counseling role was the exclusive domain of those officially labelled "school counselors."* The classroom teacher, however, has always had to deal, in one way or another, with children's problems. In today's age of anxiety, the need for the teacher to assume a counseling role is greater than ever before.

Long-term intensive formal training in counseling techniques, available in the United States in many universities and colleges and other special training facilities, is not essential for the classroom teacher. Such training alone, be it for a specialist or a classroom teacher, does not ensure that an individual will be a good counselor. More important prerequisites are a warm feeling for children and respect for their families, an ability to become aware of and understand their home environment and experiences, and an ability to listen to other persons before giving an opinion.

The teacher/counselor has a complex and difficult role. He or she should have sufficient sensitivity to be able to obtain an impression of the child's

---

*Many schools do not have school or guidance counselors because trained personnel and/or the money to pay them is nonexistent. But even if specially trained school people are available, the teacher is not relieved of the counseling role. The teacher must work with the child for many hours each day for most of the year. The teacher's ability to help the child cope with his problems on a daily basis is, in most cases, the strongest factor in determining the success of therapy.

Professional preparation of both teachers and school counselors should include effective ways of communicating with each other and ways in which they can most effectively work together to help the child.

feelings and attitudes from stance and gestures, drawings and conversations, compositions and play behavior, as well as from words. He or she must maintain rapport so that the child will express his worries whenever he feels threatened. He or she must be a good and patient listener and must be careful to avoid increasing stress on either the child or parents through his or her responses. The teacher/counselor must also provide support in the course of helping children and parents find new solutions to difficult situations.

In some school districts counseling services have been augmented by group counseling and therapeutic discussion groups conducted with children. Increasingly, the leading of such groups has become the responsibility of classroom teachers, who should have considerable preparation and be trained and supervised by, or at least have regular consultations with, a trained psychologist or psychiatrist. The professional literature provides numerous suggestions for conducting these sessions. W. Glasser [9, 10], for example, has devised procedures for groups whose aim is to help students become more responsible, more goal-directed, and better able to monitor their own growth.

What must be avoided assiduously in group counseling is probing too deeply into the feelings of children in a group situation. For example, if children discuss their anger at their parents or disclose the private affairs of their parents before a group, they may arouse feelings of great anxiety or guilt in themselves and in the others. Intimate matters should be discussed by the children only in an intimate situation.

One of the most frequent temptations that beset those counseling children is to take sides in family conflicts or to blame parents without adequate consideration of their difficulties. Parents deserve the same kind of understanding as their children. Their behavior is to a great degree the result of positive and negative experiences during their own formative years as well as the result of the current pressures upon them. They, too, have to be understood and assisted rather than blamed. Of course, in cases of poor handling of the child the teacher should intervene whenever he or she can helpfully do so. In extreme cases, such as those involving child abuse, it may be necessary to seek the intervention of other authorities.

The many roles of the teacher, and particularly the counseling role, require a high degree of moral courage. All too often teachers are directed by forces, including community standards and demands, that do not help the child to develop optimally. Too frequently these forces exert unhealthy pressures on the child and serve to impede his development. The teacher's own biases, many resulting from childhood experiences, also interfere, consciously and unconsciously, with the teacher's prime obligation in the classroom—the well-being of each student. The ability of many teachers to transcend personal biases and to display a high degree of moral courage is demonstrated by the many creative, fulfilled adults who were helped by such teachers in their early years.

THE COMMUNITY–SCHOOL RELATIONSHIP

In the past, school and parents have fulfilled distinct and separate roles in the growing child's life. The school dealt with cognitive areas and academic skills, the home taught practical skills and dealt with the child's social and emotional life, while other institutions in the community such as the church dealt with moral development and social behavior. Although life cannot be so neatly trisected, the arrangement worked relatively well as long as all of those dealing with the child shared the same values and as long as the society remained relatively stable and traditional. With accelerating social change, the role definitions began to break down, and the institutions themselves changed.

Today all of those concerned with children must interact with each other more. This must be accomplished through more communication and cooperation. Roles of parents, teachers, and community institutions overlap, and all must deal with the "whole" child. Under these circumstances continuous communication and collaboration on the child's behalf are necessary. There must be recognition that each has a related role in nurturing the child. It is not enough for parents to come to school once or twice a year to receive a "report" on the child. Instead, parents and teachers need to pool concerns, ideas, and information so that each may relate to and work with the child more effectively.

This greater involvement from both sides not only benefits the child, it also helps to provide a more positive appreciation of school programs and lessens parent anxiety about any changes that might be taking place.

Anxiety and suspicion persist in most school-community relationships. For too long parents have felt unwelcome in schools. For too long parents have come to school only for ritual conferences, an occasional PTA meeting, or a "requested" visit by the principal regarding some questionable bheavior or work habits on the part of the child. The schools have generally followed a practice of parental exclusion and maintained an attitude of "leave the teaching to us," which too frequently have resulted in mistrust, suspicion, and just plain lack of interest on the part of parents.

Changes in home–school relations, therefore, are contingent upon new attitudes by parents and the school and new forms of communicating. Formal group meetings do not provide an answer because they tend to be one-way avenues of communication. In addition, they are not part of everyone's life style, and too many parents do not attend them. One of the best ways to foster mutual respect between parents and teachers, and thus good parent–school relations, is to involve the parents directly in the school. This can be achieved in innumerable pleasurable and helpful ways, such as parents escorting students on field trips, being classroom aides, raising funds for supplementary equipment or field trips through potluck suppers, bake sales, or bazaars, running toy or clothing exchanges, acting as interpreters or tutors for children for whom

English is a second language, tutoring (when the parent has the requisite skills), coaching an athletic activity—to mention only a few of the available options. A very rewarding and educational experience for all is to have parents present a talk or demonstration to a class about their vocation, their hobby, or their travel experiences. They might even teach the class how to use a camera, for example, if photography is their vocation or hobby. On the agenda for the future might be lounges as informal meeting places for parents and teachers where coffee is always available and the atmosphere is relaxed. There might be a child-care room for parents to leave young children while they are working at the school; care might be provided by older youngsters under the guidance of a teacher as part of a curriculum to help teach young people about children.

The descriptions in Chapter 6 of the innovative programs initiated in Hartford, Connecticut, and Compton, California, are two excellent examples of parent involvement and the establishment of good community–school relations.

SUMMARY

The anxieties and deprivations with which so many children live today make the nurturing role of the school essential if the children are to grow into self-fulfilled adults. The classroom organization must meet the children's needs for self-initiated activities and communication. The physical environment should be warm and attractive. Teaching methods and classroom management procedures should focus on individual needs. The teacher's counseling role is vital to helping children express their feelings and to helping both them and their parents find solutions to their problems, while at the same time mutually supportive school and community relationships enable school personnel and parents to focus on each child's total well-being.

REFERENCES

1. Ramsauer J, quoted in Allen MR: Personal Recollections. University of California at Davis
2. Bandura A: The role of modeling processes in personality development in the young child, in Hartup W, Smothergill N (eds): Reviews of Research. Washington, D.C., National Association for the Education of Young Children, 1967
3. Mackworth JF: Some models of the reading process: Learners and skilled readers. Reading Res Q 7:701–733, 1972
4. Weber L: Toward the finer specificity, in Evaluation Reconsidered. New York, The Workshop Center for Open Education, 1973

5. Gellert J: Systematic observations: A method in child study, in Binter AR, Frey SH (eds): The Psychology of the Elementary School Child. Chicago, Rand McNally, 1972

6. Gordon IJ: Observing from a perceptual viewpoint, in Binter AR, Frey SH (eds): The Psychology of the Elementary School Child. Chicago, Rand McNally, 1972

7. Carini PF: Observation and Description: An Alternative Methodology for the Investigation of Human Phenomena. Grand Forks, North Dakota Study Group on Alternative Evaluation, University of North Dakota, 1975

8. Engel BS: A Handbook on Documentation. Grand Forks, North Dakota Study Group on Evaluation, University of North Dakota, 1975

9. Glasser W: Reality Therapy. New York, Harper & Row, 1965

10. Glasser W : Schools Without Failure. New York, Harper & Row, 1969

5

Alternative Educational Approaches

Let the main object of this, our Didactic, be as follows: To seek and to find a method of instruction, by which teachers may teach less, but learners may learn more; by which schools may be the scene of less noise, aversion, and useless labour, but of more leisure, enjoyment, and solid progress; and through which the Christian community may have less darkness, perplexity, and dissension, but on the other hand more light, orderliness, peace, and rest.

John Amos Comenius, c. 1660 [1, iii]

Educational ferment exists the world over as nations struggle with problems of change. The study of innovative programs of all countries will enrich every teacher's repertoire of strategies and his or her understanding of the goals of education as they relate to different cultures.

Of particular interest are programs in England, the Soviet Union, China, and Israel. Although social conditions and political convictions may differ in these countries, much of what is being done educationally can be adapted in the United States and elsewhere, for tasks of educators are similar in all countries. Careful assessment of the needs of the child, monitoring the progress of each child, application of modern theoretical findings in the areas that influence learning and instruction, and respect for the child are the ingredients found in all effective educational programs regardless of country of origin.

However, areas of emphasis and priority may differ. For instance, reports from China emphasize the absence of fighting or other unfriendly contacts among the students, responsibility for all members of the group, and the mutual respect of teachers and students [2]. Reports from the Soviet Union emphasize the carefully worked-out methods used in the education of children with learning difficulties, the careful screening of all children at 3 years of age, and the seriousness and interest with which children pursue their educational goals [3].

In Israel the results of close interaction among children in a kibbutz group, as well as the positive effects of their participation in and identification with adult endeavors, has long been known [4]. In addition, Israelis face the need of providing an educational system for an immigrant nation whose members speak a number of languages and come from highly disparate backgrounds. Imaginative attempts to solve these problems are worth studying.

The development in England since World War II of infant and junior schools operating on the principles of the integrated day or open scheme has had an enormous impact on education.* Such schools have been a major inspiration for the flowering in the United States of many different versions of what is commonly called the "open classroom." If we look at open-classroom ideas as approaches and philosophies rather than as embodied in a rigid model known as *The Open Classroom,* they have much to offer many teachers in many situations.

In the United States the rising demands in the 1960s for social and racial justice as exemplified in the civil rights movement and the war on poverty were reflected in education's concern for compensatory and early childhood education. Head Start programs proliferated, differing in philosophy and curricula but all stating their purpose as that of enabling preschool children from disadvantaged backgrounds to enter regular public school on a par with their more advantaged peers. The Head Start programs aroused public awareness of the prerequisites for academic learning, the need for increased medical and social services, and the benefits of direct parental and community involvement in education.

Most of the initial short-run reports on the effectiveness of Head Start were favorable. Nevertheless, when follow-up studies began to appear in the early 1970s, it became evident that gains made by the 4-year-olds in Head Start programs were being lost as they progressed through kindergarten and the primary grades. Consequently, Project Follow-Through was instituted, with federal funding, to serve the same populations served by Head Start. Project Follow-Through was designed to create at least some fundamental changes within the public schools themselves. This Project and the open classroom will be described as examples of innovative programs in the United States.

---

*British children begin formal schooling at the age of 5-plus and remain in the infant school through the age of 7. The junior schools serve children of ages 8 through 11.

PROJECT FOLLOW-THROUGH

In a small but most informative booklet, *Experiments in Primary Education: Aspects of Project Follow-Through* by Eleanor E. Maccoby and Miriam Zellner [5], the goals of ten Follow-Through programs are discussed. At first glance the goals of the program sponsors appear to be different. For instance, self-direction is a major goal of David Armington, who sponsors the Follow-Through model of the Educational Development Center in Newton, Massachusetts. He states that "a fundamental educational aim for children is to assume responsibility for their own learning" [5, p 6]. In contrast, the Engelmann-Becker program (The Department of Educational Psychology at the University of Illinois in Urbana) starts with the premise that disadvantaged children are academically behind middle-class children. The conclusion is that "the primary concern of a compensatory program is to teach academic skills" [5, p 7]. The curriculum of the Florida project (The College of Education at the University of Florida in Gainesville), sponsored by Ira Gordon, is described as having an "orientation toward the theories of Jean Piaget. The children learn to arrange items in series, to classify and to name" [5, p 12].

A closer look shows that the divergent goals stated by the ten projects are usually not the only ones; in practice the programs embody several integrated goals. It may be that the sponsors emphasized one specific goal so as to underline the uniqueness of their project. Maccoby and Zellner state, "Indeed a program's potential advantages probably *must* be exaggerated if it is to have a chance of adoption in the first place" [5, p 128].

The main objectives put forth by the different sponsors can be divided into three groups: (1) self-direction and school behavior, (2) academic learning, and (3) training in the skills underlying academic progress, such as language, perception, memory, higher cognitive functions, and social and emotional growth. These objectives are interrelated and have to be taken into account by any teacher; thus, even though the stated goals seem to express divergent aims, many of the educational practices of the various projects are similar.

Maccoby and Zellner conclude that two main psychological theories have influenced the Follow-Through projects. The first is *reinforcement theory* (behavior modification). The adherents of this theory set as a goal effecting changes in observable behavior. The second is *cognitive developmental theory* (usually that of Piaget) whose proponents set as their main goal the cognitive growth of the child or the interrelationship between cognitive and social-emotional growth.

Commonalities in Follow-Through Projects

In spite of the differences emphasized by the program leaders, both kinds of programs, those based on behavior modification and those emphasizing cognitive development, showed many commonalities. All taught vocabulary and the relationship concepts of time and space (up, down, further, nearer, later, earlier, and so on). Praise and approval were important to build good self-images and foster improvement. Maccoby and Zellner report that the children in the programs they surveyed were enthusiastic, happy, and excited. Educators, regardless of approach, agree on what not to use: punishment, coercion, nagging, scolding, or anything that could arouse anxiety or self-depreciation in the child. Inattentive or disruptive behavior was usually regarded as a consequence, not as the cause, of poor learning. In nearly all programs the children were encouraged to take responsibility for order in their classroom. Development of self-esteem was an important goal in all programs.

In none of the ten projects were severe behavior problems observed. In all programs the enthusiasm of the teachers and their committment to assisting the children was very high, and in all programs the progress of the children was carefully monitored so that intervention could take place before failure occurred. Feedback was considered important in most programs.

These commonalities pointed out by Maccoby and Zellner are of great value for educators. The finding of these critical variables can certainly guide those seeking to make schools better places for children to be.

THE OPEN CLASSROOM

Although the open classrooms as we know them owe much to recent innovations largely based on the work of Piaget, they have a long history. In the early part of the twentieth century John Dewey proposed activity-based (and experience-based) schools, emphasizing flexible curricula in which the process was regarded as important as the product and interaction was encouraged between the children and the teacher. Dewey, too, was concerned with preparing children to live in an ever changing world:

> It is necessary to prepare the coming generation for a new and more just and humane society which is sure to come and which, unless hearts and minds are prepared by education, is likely to come attended with all the evils that result from social changes effected by violence [6, p 129].

Unfortunately, we have not really heeded Dewey's warning.

Maria Montessori, working in Italy in the last years of the nineteenth century and the first decade of the twentieth century, recommended freeing children from rigid curricula and stultifying classroom conditions:

> We know only too well the sorry spectacle of the teacher who, in the ordinary schoolroom, must pour certain cut and dried facts into the heads

of the scholars. In order to succeed in this barren task, she finds it necessary to discipline her pupils into immobility and to force their attention. Prizes and punishment are ever-ready and efficient aids to the master who must force into a given attitude of mind and body those who are condemned to be his listeners [7, p 21].

In contrast, "the school must permit the *free, natural manifestations of the child* if scientific pedagogy is to be born in the school" [7, p 15].

Most of all, it is Piaget who has given renewed impetus to the search for more effective and enlightened approaches to education:

> Piaget's contribution is not in developing new educational ideas, but in providing a vast body of data and theory which provide a sound basis for a "progressive" approach to the schools. A long time ago, John Dewey, in rejecting traditional approaches to education, called for and attempted to provide a "philosophy of experience"; that is, a thorough explication of the ways in which children make use of experience in genuine learning. Piaget has gone a long way toward meeting this need [8, p 231].

The open classroom is designed to serve the child rather than the school system. It does this by providing a setting in which any child, regardless of abilities, interest, temperament, or background, can achieve his or her optimum development socially, emotionally, cognitively, and physically. The open classroom is characterized by a flexible layout and the availability of a wide range of materials, any of which children may use in pursuing their individual interests. Generally, the children are permitted to move around freely in the room. Often they work independently, in groups of two or more; at other times they share in activities for the class as a whole.

The aim is to provide a natural environment that stimulates development and enables each child to work at his or her own level and pace—no pressure forces work on tasks for which the child lacks the necessary developmental ability. The teaching of skills is "open-ended"; that is, each child goes as far as his or her abilities and interests permit. The children may not be grouped strictly according to age; the ages in a class often vary by up to three years (family or vertical grouping). The atmosphere is cooperative rather than competitive; the children are encouraged to inspect each other's work, to learn from each other, and to help each other.

Within this general framework the term "open classroom" can refer to a variety of approaches and settings. For example, it may refer to a setting in which more than 100 children interact in a central classroom, with bays in which the different groups spend part of the time (the open-space classroom). Or the open classroom may reflect a setting in which the children direct most of their own studies. Whatever the structure, the open classroom is designed to provide the child with the opportunity to use natural drives to explore and create. The child learns to solve problems by seeing and finding out how things and ideas work and how they are related to each other. He attacks problems from various angles with the variety of materials at his disposal. He is involved in the learning process as an active participant. Programmed material and step-by-step linear progression in learning may be used selectively, but the steps follow the child's developmental growth as well as the structure of the subject matter.

Much learning occurs through the integration of experiences. For example, the child may learn from a story that a whale is very big; later, that it is not a fish; later that whales have been used and misused for human purposes. He may inspect a model of a whale and find out how it breathes. The child may learn by keeping a notebook, by reading books or newspaper articles, by seeing films, by viewing slides, drawings, or panoramas in a museum, by making a chart showing the relative sizes of animals, by constructing a model, by drawing a map of the migratory routes of whales, or by acting out a sea voyage. The teacher helps the child to integrate and interrelate these learning experiences and takes every opportunity to enrich the child's concepts—of whales, sealife, mammals, ecology, for example—so that the child achieves an increasingly coherent and cohesive picture of the world.

Integrating experiences and building concepts in this way is a characteristic of all good teaching. It is the bias of some educators, among them this author, that it is most easily achieved within the context of the open classroom, where each child has the freedom to explore for himself or herself the various aspects of the subjects of each one's interest.

The Role of the Teacher

In traditional education the role of the teacher is quite well defined. The teacher has learned prescribed sequences of skills and content, which are then more or less forcibly conveyed to the children. The philosophy has tended to be "Ram it in, ram it in. Children's heads are hollow" [9]. In open classrooms the teacher's role is more varied and less directive, but no less involved. Well-conducted open classrooms bring active adults together with active children [10]. That is to say, the teacher's role is neither passive nor simple. As Figure 5–1 indicates, in comparing the teacher's role in different models of education, the contribution of both teacher and child in the open classroom is high.

Much of the teacher's active involvement occurs when the children are not present in the classroom. Then the teacher works to create an inviting and varied environment that is organized around children's interests and contains materials for discovery learning and creative activities as well as learning skills and content. Much careful planning and evaluation is required of the teacher (or

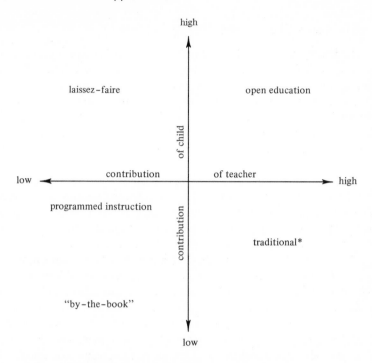

*In the original figure this category is labeled "traditional British."

Fig. 5–1.   Double classification scheme based on the extent to which (1) the individual teacher and (2) the individual child are active contributors to decisions regarding the content and process of learning. (Modified from Anne Bussis and Edward A. Chittenden, *Analysis of an Approach to Open Education*. Princeton, N.J., Educational Testing Howie, 1970.)

of the team if it is a cooperative teaching situation) to set up an effective environment that is conducive to participation for all children in the classroom.

When the children are present, the teacher must help coordinate the varied activities taking place, consult with individual children about their work, teach small group lessons, help children find ways to solve problems (both socially and intellectually), motivate children who are at loose ends, encourage and contribute to any exciting new interests or investigations that emerge, move children to higher levels of thought and inquiry through questions and comments, praise good work, give support to those who need it, make observations, and, through it all, enjoy the school day and find it as much of a learning experience as do the children. It is an exciting, exacting, role, which is often tiring but never boring.

Why Open Classrooms Sometimes Fail

The history of experiments with the open classroom system is not one of total success. There have been a number of instances of failure. The main reason for the failure is pinpointed in the booklet, *Open Plan Primary Schools* [11]: the diversity within the open classroom means that it requires much underlying organization and structure, unobtrusive though this may be. The authors of this English survey doubt whether "a teacher chronically weak in organization and control can be of much help in these open surroundings" [11, p 3].

There are other causes of difficulties that need to be noted. A teacher may fail because he or she is accustomed to the authoritarian role of the teacher traditionally characteristic of the conventional classroom. Without a spirit of cooperation between teacher and students an open classroom cannot function. In the open classroom the children model themselves on their teacher. Modeling is a necessary educational method whenever behavior modification is not the main approach to classroom discipline. But the necessary degree of cooperation can only be achieved in such a setting if the teacher treats the children with the same degree of helpfulness, cooperation, and respect that she expects the children to show to her and to each other. In an open classroom the children and the teacher must be sensitive and responsive to each other's needs.

Failure also occurs where there are strict age-grade requirements. The open classroom structure cannot be achieved when children are afraid of failing. Progress in achievement in literacy and numerical skills should certainly be evaluated, but achievement has to be measured as rate of growth and not as age-grade norms. The reason for this is that all children do not learn at the same rate. Some children learn to decipher printed material effortlessly before they enter kindergarten; others may not do so before 7 or 8 years of age. Children will make more progress if they are permitted to proceed at a rate that is within their scope, instead of being expected to conform to a norm.

In order to avoid pitfalls inherent in instituting open education, change must be undertaken gradually with careful planning and communication and a considerable infusion of resources and time. Parents, children, teachers, and community need to be carefully prepared to provide mutual assistance [12].

PROGRAM EVALUATION

Program evaluation is often given insufficient attention. It is, however, of crucial importance for the survival of any and all kinds of innovative educational programs.

At the present time a few popular reading tests provide the primary vehicles for determining educational success. Reading tests not only lead to emphasis of a very small part of the program but, in themselves, have a number of serious flaws. Most have major cultural biases with respect to content, style, and instructions [13]. Many, especially in the early grades during the period of reading acquisition, are valid only if the children are using a specific reading approach; for example, the Metropolitan Reading Test has content validity only for a basal reader approach. Worst of all, the emphasis placed on these tests will frequently "drive schools and teachers into adopting pressure-cooker programs to meet the needs of tests, not children" [13].

It is essential that evaluations be based on far broader criteria. We must use a number of techniques and instruments to give a multifaceted view of what is really going on in a program or classroom. Skills should continue to be measured, either by normative tests or by the use of criterion-referenced checklists. Evaluation of reading skills should be augmented by observations of how much and what children read when given free time to do so. Concept formation and problem solving may be measured by tests such as the Boehm Test of Basic Concepts or by somewhat more informal scales such as Let's Look at Children [14] or by observation of children in prearranged problem-solving situations [15]. Important areas such as classroom atmosphere and management may be illuminated by using rating scales and other procedures like those discussed by B. Rosenshine and N. Furst [16]. Videotapes of classrooms can be made and shown to independent observers who will evaluate them using a rating scale developed to show desirable behaviors (cooperative work, on-task behavior, asking for help when needed, replacing materials, group participation, and so forth). Teachers' records and children's work should always be a part of any program evaluation.

An evaluation based on such a balanced and comprehensive group of measures and observations would give a realistic view of a program to those making decisions about it. Such a report could also be used for giving information about the program to interested persons, such as parents, because of the wide-ranging amount of information and descriptive content it involves.

Those interested in these kinds of evaluation problems will find the publications of the North Dakota Study Group on Alternative Evaluation* especially helpful.

REFERENCES

1. Keatinge MN (ed): The Greate Didactic of John Amos Comenius. London, Adam and Charles Black, 1896

*One can obtain information about evaluation by writing to the North Dakota Study Group on Alternative Evaluation, Center for Teaching and Learning, University of North Dakota, Grand Forks, North Dakota.

2. National Academy of Sciences, Committee on Scholarly Communication with the People's Republic of China, Early Childhood Development Delegation. Kindergartens. Washington, D.C., the Academy, 1974 (mimeo)

3. Caldwell BM: Personal communication, 1974

4. Spiro ME: Children of the Kibbutz. New York, Schocken, 1966

5. Maccoby EE, Zellner M: Experiments in Primary Education: Aspects of Project Follow-Through. New York, Harcourt, 1970

6. Dewey J: Progressive education and the science of education, in Silberman CE (ed): The Open Classroom Reader. New York, Vintage, 1973

7. Montessori M: The Montessori Method (George AE, transl). New York, Schocken, 1964

8. Ginsberg H, Opper S: Piaget's Theory of Intellectual Development. Englewood Cliffs, N.J., Prentice-Hall, 1969

9. Randazzo JD, Arnold JM: Does open education really work in an urban setting? Phi Delta Kappan 53:107–110, 1972

10. Bussis A, Chittenden EA: Analysis of an approach to open education. Princeton. N. J., Educational Testing Service, 1970

11. Department of Education and Science, Great Britain: Open Plan Primary Schools. Education Survey 16. London, Her Majesty's Stationery Office, 1972

12. Taylor J: Organizing the Open Classroom. New York, Schocken, 1972

13. Meier D: Reading failure and the tests, a paper for the Workshop Center for Open Education, New York, 1973

14. Board of Education, City of New York. Let's Look at Children. Princeton, N.J., Educational Testing Service, 1965

15. Duckworth E: Evaluating African science: Case in point, in Evaluation Reconsidered. New York, Workshop Center for Open Education, 1973

16. Rosenshine B, Furst N: The use of direct observation to study teaching, in Travers R (ed): Second Handbook of Research on Teaching. Chicatgo, Rand McNally, 1973

6

Two Examples of Innovative Programs

> *If education were conducted as a process of fullest utilization of present resources, liberating and guiding capacities that are now urgent, it goes without saying that the lives of the young would be much richer in meaning than they are now.*
>
> *John Dewey* [1, p 270]

Two innovative programs in the United States—the Hartford (Connecticut) open education program and the Compton (California) project—will be described in this chapter. The Hartford program wrought major changes in the city's educational procedures. Its success owes much to its gradual, intelligent initiation. The Compton project, a more limited undertaking with more restricted goals, illustrates how relatively small changes can make large differences in the lives of children. It is hoped that these accounts will provide helpful insights for teachers and administrators interested in initiating similar innovations in their school curricula.

THE HARTFORD PROGRAM*

The city of Hartford in the state of Connecticut is a highly diverse city of nearly 200,000 people. It has 25 elementary schools and 3 high schools. Within

---

*The description of the Hartford program has been written by Ann-Marie Miller, resource teacher in Hartford. A further account of the program has been provided by Randazzo and Arnold [2].

the 25 elementary schools nearly 40 different languages are spoken, ranging from Portuguese to Ukranian. Of these, there are at least six major language groups. The largest of the non–English-speaking groups is Spanish-speaking; the majority of this group is made up of Puerto Ricans, but there are also members of the Peruvian, Bolivian, and Cuban communities.*

The city is also heterogeneous in its economic mix. The children attending public schools range from those who come from wealthy and highly sophisticated families to very many others whose families subsist on welfare. Further, there is a great deal of mobility within the city itself.

Hartford, in other words, is the kind of heterogeneous place that in the not too distant past would have been called a typical melting pot. Today it is quite clear that the citizens of Hartford have no intention of melting; indeed, they are proud of their various ethnic identities. The citizens believe that the public schools should serve and teach all the children, respecting the individuality of each child and the right of each to maintain ethnic identities, traits, and language. At the same time the schools are expected to provide each child with the skills and knowledge necessary to function in a highly technological, predominantly English-speaking society.

These are certainly major challenges for a school system, and for a long time they seemed impossible to meet. Hartford public schools tried to solve their problems in the standard ways by having more curriculum meetings, more teacher training, and more teacher aides; but all of the efforts seemed to result in very little headway. The educational authorities, therefore, began to look for a more radical solution. It was becoming clear that the usual teacher-centered classroom simply would not work when many of the children could not understand the teacher, when the levels were so disparate, and the heterogeneity was so enormous.

The superintendent of schools in Hartford in 1966, Medill Bair, invited Joseph Randazzo, a talented innovator with experience and training both in Montessori schools and American public schools, to introduce and implement more radical changes. Under Randazzo's guidance a new approach was initiated in the elementary schools that combined aspects of the Montessori classroom with those of the British Infant School.** A Montessori base is now used in terms of management and of basic skill sequences, with ideas adapted from the open-classroom system of Great Britain utilized to provide enrichment, variety, cultural content, and language and literacy training.

Most of the classrooms are self-contained, with about 30 children in each. The classrooms have the characteristics of open classrooms, but they are not

---

*Bilingual classrooms, based on the same principles as other Hartford primary rooms, meet the needs of children for whom Spanish is the dominant tongue.

**It should be emphasized that much of the success of the program has been due to the expertise of its first director and to the considerable support he enjoyed from the superintendent of schools and from the board of education.

open-space classrooms with the exception of two new schools. Hartford has many old schools, and no funds are available for architectural renovation. However, open classrooms and open education seem to work quite as well in a school built in 1920 as in one built in 1975.

For each classroom a rich variety of materials is provided in all the major sense modalities so that the children can learn not only at their own levels but also in their own way. The range of materials within any given classroom is extensive, covering two, three, or even more years of learning. Therefore, a child can be placed at his own level whenever he arrives, whether at the beginning of the year or in the middle. Since the teacher is no longer dependent upon the quietness of the classroom for success in teaching, a newly arrived child can be assigned to another child to teach him the classroom rules and help him find his materials.

The teacher finds the child's level of achievement in various areas through the use of simple diagnostic tests. The child's progress is noted on a checklist as he proceeds; should he move to another school within the city, the checklist is sent with him so that the next teacher knows what he has learned and how he learned it.

Initiating the Program

Change in a public school must begin with the key person who is most involved with the children—the classroom teacher. *Every* primary Hartford teacher was asked to participate in a workshop program, which was conducted over a period of three years. At various times each teacher attended three-week training sessions; substitute teachers took over the regular classrooms.

When the program was introduced each primary classroom was allotted $800 worth of teaching materials, a necessary step because many Hartford classrooms had previously been bare of anything but textbooks, blackboards, chalk, paper, and pencils. An aide was also hired for each primary room, with the classroom teacher participating in the selection. The aide came from the immediate neighborhood served by the school. If a particular foreign language group predominated, an attempt was made to find an aide who spoke the language. The aide also participated in the training sessions. In most class-rooms the "teachers" are not identified as either head teacher or an aide.

Winning Community Approval

The success of any public school program depends on the support of the community. From the beginning, the leaders of the program took the community's feelings into account. The changes sought by the program were indeed major; certainly the classrooms that are its outcome in no way resemble those that the parents themselves attended. Because it was assumed that many parents would feel confused, possibly even angry, about the innovations, attempts were made to keep in constant communication with the community and gain its consent as the changes were gradually instituted. Randazzo and other members of his staff spoke as frequently as possible to various Parent-Teacher Associations and other groups within the community. Newspaper and other media coverage was sought to describe and explain the program.

Parents were encouraged to visit the classrooms as they opened. Teachers and principals tried hard to make the parents feel comfortable and welcome, and the school personnel took as much time as necessary to answer questions. Perhaps parental visits were the most important part of community acceptance, for *seeing* what was going on made a big difference. The comment most often heard from parents was, "If only it had been like this when I went to school!"

Much care had to be taken to ensure that the parents did not assume that because school was a pleasant place, no learning occurred there. Learning activities were explained carefully to both parents and children and were always referred to as work, not play.

To introduce the program to the community only one classroom was opened, but it was opened with some fanfare. One of the best teachers* in the system was chosen to direct the children. Visitors were encouraged to attend class, and the classroom made a great impression. Other schools were attracted to the idea, and they requested that they have similar "models" in their buildings. In the following year five more classrooms were opened. These were all carefully evaluated, and community approval was found to be considerable.

The aides were an important component in winning community approval. Unlike the teachers, they came from the neighborhoods themselves and could thus answer questions about the school over a cup of coffee, while taking a walk, or at an evening party. After school hours the aides became unpaid ambassadors of the exciting new program in Hartford's primary classrooms.

The Physical Layout of the Open Classroom

As for the classrooms themselves, they vary greatly; some are noisier, some quieter, some with more group activities, some with less, for within the broad perimeters that the model prescribes the teachers are always encouraged to find a combination of practices that suits their individual temperaments and teaching styles as well as the characteristics of their students.

Nevertheless, there are certain common factors. Most of the classrooms are divided into learning centers or areas. These may be used for such activities as math, language, social studies, science, and art. Somewhere in each room an area is made available in which the entire class can gather for meetings. In

*Ms. Jean Gelormino.

general, such sessions occur one to three times each day. They are important for stimulating class discussion, motivating the children, and assuring the group feeling so essential to the functioning of a successful classroom.

Every room also provides a comfortable area for quiet reading, often brightly decorated, furnished with rugs, pillows, and a multitude of carefully selected and attractive books. When sufficient money is available, the classrooms also contain a listening center equipped with tape recorders, Language Masters, record players, junction boxes, and earphones.

Each learning area in the room contains a great variety of materials, some permanently assigned to the area and others there for a limited time. Those there on a "temporary" basis are changed frequently. Many of the materials might be familiar to elementary classrooms anywhere—phonics bingo, worksheets laminated for permanence, counters, word wheels, flash cards, and so on. Other materials might seem exotic and less familiar—for example, a variety of balances, teacher-made books, collections of interesting manufactured and natural objects (including shells, stones, bird nests, plants), sand trays, art materials of various kinds, and all sorts of recycled objects. Some of the materials are contributed by the children and reflect their interests, such as books that they have written and illustrated, home-invented learning games (some of which prove to be very difficult to play), and interesting objects that they have brought to be shared, admired, and learned about.

The rooms are carefully planned in terms of traffic management so that the children move smoothly from one activity to another. The children do not have their own desks; they work in the various work areas, close to the equipment they need. When they finish an activity, it is checked by the teacher or the aide. The child then carefully returns the materials used. This can be done easily and efficiently because the materials are in containers that are easily carried and both the containers and their places on the shelves are color-coded and symbol-coded. The child needs only to match the color-coded symbol on the material to that on the shelf to return it to its proper place. In order to make this system work, a vast amount of shelf space must be provided; most rooms have homemade bookcases, usually constructed from pine boards and cinder block. The bookcases are used not only to display materials but also to define traffic paths and the perimeters of learning areas.

Because children do not have their own desks, they are assigned cubbyholes or mail boxes in which to keep their personal possessions. However, most material is owned in common; this eliminates the squabbles over ownership that often characterize regular classrooms ("I've got a broken red crayon in my box, and he doesn't. I want one just like his.") Crayons, for example, are just put in boxes according to color. When a child needs one, he helps himself, returning it when he is finished.

Children's work is displayed attractively around the room and treated with care and respect by teachers and children alike. Because children are working at different levels and in different ways, no display ever consists of rows of more-or-less identical papers.

Respect is paid to children's work in the positive feedback provided by teachers and classmates when a child's best efforts are shown. This helps to create a climate of high expectation, which contributes greatly to continued learning and the production of work of high achievement.

Classroom Rules

A room so rich in materials, activities, and people must have a carefully structured set of rules by which all live or chaos will ensue. The rules chosen have largely been derived from the Montessori system of management. Essentially, they are the following:

1. When a child starts an activity, he is expected to finish it or to ask for help if he cannot do it by himself. His work has to be checked, and then he returns the materials used to where he found them.
2. No child may interfere with any one else. Children are taught to respect each other's activities.
3. The children are expected to respond appropriately to designated signals from the teacher. Various signals are generally used, such as a record or music for putting away materials and lights being switched on to gain immediate attention.

Although these rules are simple, they take a great deal of getting used to and may need to be reinforced time and again.

Record Keeping

The richness, variety, and flexibility of an open classroom require a great deal of "keeping track" on the part of the teacher. With so many children doing so many things at so many different levels, the results could be skills left unlearned, problems left unsolved, and perhaps even children left untaught. These can only be prevented by a comprehensive system of record keeping and ultimately by diagnostic teaching.

The record keeping should be as simple and automatic as possible so that it will not become a burden. It must be scrupulously maintained, for the teacher's records and observations form the basis for guidance of the child's educational program.

In most classes some form of work cards are used (sometimes termed work assignments, prescriptions, or contracts). Activities that the child is asked to do are listed on the task card and checked off as they are completed. The teacher tries not to prescribe activities for more than 50 percent of a child's time. For the remainder the child is permitted to select his own activities. (Children often make wiser decisions about their learning needs than their teachers.) The freely chosen activities may be added to the list on the work card as they are completed, and the card filed as a record of the child's progress. In addition, the teacher keeps careful, brief records of observations of each child.

Individualizing Learning

In a "well-individualized" classroom, no two work cards will be the same. In such a classroom it is possible to accommodate children with learning difficulties, language impairments, or other special problems. The variety of materials available and the philosophy of individualization make it possible to prescribe activities appropriate to their needs, and the lack of competition makes it possible for children with difficulties to progress at their own rate without becoming cruelly aware of their inability to keep up with their peers. The gifted child equally is enabled to go at his or her own pace; in an open-classroom setting no longer do arbitrarily imposed class rates of progress hold back a gifted child. If the child exhausts the resources of the classroom in a certain area, permission is given to move for a period to another classroom to use materials and resources there. The child returns to his or her own age group for the remaining areas of study. It is also possible to accommodate a child who speaks a language not spoken by the teacher because the child can obtain the help of a friend who speaks the same language. In addition, the reliance upon concrete materials makes it possible to begin instruction by demonstration rather than by complicated verbal statements. A child who enters in the middle of the year does not have to attempt to achieve at the levels of the group but can start at his own level, possibly with the assistance of a more experienced child.

Current Assessment of the Program

The program has been evaluated continuously on a formal and informal basis. The attitudes and reactions of both parents and children have been given equal weight with academic progress in judging its efficacy. Results of this constant monitoring have served as the basis for decisions regarding possible changes in any aspect of the program.

Because the program was introduced gradually, only now are its "graduates" moving into the middle schools in sufficient numbers to permit evaluation of their adjustment to a more formal academic structure. The children who had experienced the open classrooms during their primary school years and who then moved into more traditional* fourth, fifth, or sixth grades evidenced no difficulties.

The cooperation of the elementary classroom teachers has been indispensable for the success of the program, and such cooperation has been given in full measure. Responses to questionnaires indicate that teachers overwhelmingly support the program and feel themselves better able to meet the needs of each child as a result of the many changes that have occurred in Hartford classrooms.

And what of the future? Vincent Rogers, one of the seminal spokesmen for constructive change in American schools, sums it up very well:

> In my judgment, Hartford's open education program is one of the most exciting, significant, and, perhaps, one of the most underrated programs of its kind in the U.S. Here is, after all, a working model of American urban child-centered or informal education succeeding on a scale that is rare both in England and the U.S. This is *not* an "experimental" program involving a few show-place schools. Ten thousand children, 350 classrooms, and more than 1,000 teachers and aides have been involved since the project's beginning six years ago. Funding has been largely local, with a minimum amount of federal support; teacher training has been, from the beginning, a major effort or thrust of the program. Hartford operates a full-blown teachers' center, includes a minimum of three weeks of full-time teacher training (or retraining) for every primary teacher and aide in the city, and provides a staff of skilled resource teachers who work out of the center and offer teachers the sustained, on-the-job help that is so often lacking in other situations. Teachers completing the training program are provided with most of the materials necessary to make such a program work initially.
>
> The Hartford program is not an unequivocal success. Some teachers go through training, work at the center, and remain unconvinced and unchanged. At the moment, budget cuts have reduced the number of resource teachers and have curtailed some of the activities of the teachers' center. At this writing [1971], however, open education is alive and well and flourishing in Hartford. Will it continue to grow and develop? This depends, to some extent, on the administration's willingness to stay with, support, and build upon an essentially sound and well thought-through educational philosophy or position—and conversely, to avoid the temptation (so common in American education) to abandon anything that has been in existence this long and go madly on to the next "innovation." [3, p 110]

---

*Many of the upper elementary classrooms also adopted the open classroom structure; however, greater emphasis was placed on the primary grades during the initial phases.

As of this writing (1976) administrative, financial, and moral support seem far from assured.

THE COMPTON PROJECT

The project undertaken in Compton, California, is an example of a readiness program designed to enhance the abilities of economically disadvantaged and culturally different children during their early school years [3]. It began with a minimum of resources and was restricted by the nature of its funding to a relatively short period of time—14 weeks. Outside consultants* and positive teacher support were used to initiate change. The project's main goal was to train the children in skills necessary for adjustment to the school situation and for academic learning. This was to be accomplished in an atmosphere of mutual trust and friendliness.

The achievement of the children in the Compton school district had been very low in previous years, and many of the children had had to repeat kindergarten, often without showing improved performance, during the following year of school attendance.

Compton, a medium-sized city in Los Angeles County, is geographically and economically a part of the Los Angeles urban complex. In contrast to Hartford, it does not have a heterogeneous population mix. In 1970, when the school project was undertaken, the population was predominantly black, with pockets of Spanish-speaking families.

Teacher Training

When school district personnel invited the Marianne Frostig Center of Educational Therapy to help enhance the program in early childhood education, they emphasized that any project had to be conducted in such a way that it could easily be reproduced and carried on by district personnel alone at the termination of the grant fourteen weeks later. It was decided that the widest beneficial influence would be to conduct demonstration classes for inservice training of teachers in day care centers, Head Start programs, and kindergarten and primary grade classes. The main emphasis was on the training of the kindergarten teachers.

The demonstration classes were held at one school on four days each week, and four kindergarten teachers were trained as resource teachers over the fourteen weeks of the project. Head Start teachers were trained separately.

*The Marianne Frostig Center of Educational Therapy in Los Angeles developed a pilot program for the 1970 spring semester of the Compton City School District. Denise Nighman was the resource training teacher, and Phyllis Maslow was the coordinator of the project.

Other teachers, nurses, aides, and administrators concerned with early childhood education observed the demonstration classes, conducted by a supervising teacher from the Frostig Center. They met later with the Frostig teacher for discussion. In addition, the Frostig teacher conducted more formal workshops once a week for the district's teaching staff concerned with early childhood education.

Winning Community Approval

Community support was invited in several ways. The initial proposal was discussed and voted on at an open meeting of the school board. The parents who attended made it very clear that they did not want their children used as "guinea pigs" for another "one-shot" project. Assured that the project was directed primarily to training district personnel and was designed ·to be carried on by Compton teachers, the board approved.

Parents of children in the demonstration classes were invited to participate in the learning experience with their own children. Only a few parents were able to attend classes, but they served as ambassadors in the community. It was particularly fortunate that a Spanish-speaking father was able to attend a few sessions; his positive feelings for the program helped insure its acceptance in his community, as did the demonstration teacher's consultations with the parish priest. The parents who came were impressed by how enthusiastic their children could be about learning. Perhaps of equal importance, the teachers were impressed with the parent interest and became more involved themselves.

Demonstration Classes

The program required no major curriculum changes or changes in class organization. A demonstration lesson for one hour was given twice a week during the regular session of each of the two afternoon kindergarten classes. The four kindergarten teachers observed. They were helped during later discussions to integrate the program into their regular classroom curriculum. Special emphasis was put on the incorporation of creative movement and body awareness exercises into daily physical education and playground periods. The theoretical basis of movement education program is found in this author's book, *Movement Education* [5].

The children and teachers responded enthusiastically. At the beginning of the project the children preferred to spend most of the time using large toys and playing games; many could not hold a pencil or crayon correctly; few spoke in complete sentences. After only fourteen weeks the children seemed much more aware and curious; they talked more, and in more complex sentences, about classroom tasks; many were able, with a great deal of pride, to write two- and three-letter words from dictation. Nearly all had learned to write numbers and the letters of the alphabet.

The four kindergarten teachers selected for the pilot were interested, cooperative, and dedicated, and during their training period they utilized the program in a flexible and intelligent way. At the end of the fourteen weeks all four were prepared to act as demonstration and resource teachers with minimal supervision. They reported that they had acquired greater belief in, and expectations concerning, the learning potentials of their students.

Program Evaluation

The scores from the only standardized test administered to the children participating strongly support the observations of the children's gains in learning. During the first week of the project the children were given the Boehm Test of Basic Concepts [6], which is designed to measure children's mastery of concepts necessary for following directions and assimilating academic instructions. These are concepts designating position in space and spatial relationships (inside, between, bottom, and so on), quantity (some, few, most), time (before, after), and other relationships (different, same, other). The mean class scores, in relation to middle socioeconomic norms, were at the fifteenth, fifty-fifth, nineteenth and tenth percentiles. When the test was given again at the end of the pilot, the mean class scores were at the sixtieth, sixtieth, eightieth, and fifty-fifth percentile for middle socioeconomic norms; if low socioeconomic means are used, all four classes scored above the ninetieth percentile.

Program Content

The Frostig readiness program *Pictures and Patterns* [7] was the core of the school program. Although the emphasis in this program is on visual perceptual skills, the total program, however, is designed to prepare the child for academic learning (1) by helping him acquire basic learning abilities (for example, sensory-motor functions, receptive and expressive language, auditory and visual perception, certain instructional concepts) (2) and by helping him integrate his basic abilities and apply them in learning academic skills and content. Basic mathematical concepts (set, cardinal and ordinal numbers, numerals, number facts, and so on) and beginning decoding skills (sounds of the alphabet, reading and writing of three- and four-letter phonetically spelled words, and so on) were also taught.

Worksheets from *Pictures and Patterns* [7] served as the focus for each lesson plan, but they were never used in isolation. Actual lesson plans used in the Compton project are presented in the Appendix to this chapter. Their tabular form was set by the granting agency, and the details included only indicate the materials used and the skills trained. These lessons illustrate how training in a variety of abilities and academic skills can be integrated in each lesson, using a visual perception training sheet as the focus. Each lesson was given to 15 kindergarten children. The lessons were structured in such a way that the teacher could easily check each response, and concrete experiences were closely associated or integrated with verbal experiences. Many of the responses required physical movement.

Conclusion

The brief description of the content of the Compton program does not mirror the total effort of the involved personnel nor the totality of its aspects. The cancer gnawing on the subsociety of the black population is mistrust—a mistrust that is expressed in the behavior of the children, a mistrust that retards their progress. The monosyllabic responses of many black children, their seeming lack of ideas, their passivity, their lack of enthusiasm to learn may —and often does—lead to the erroneous conclusion that they have low intelligence or communicative ability. The Compton program in this instance elicited quite different reactions from the children. The movement education, music, storytelling, play acting, and similar activities, as well as the structured instruction in perceptual skills, basic concepts, and fundamentals of language, were carried on in a spirit of joyful working together and respect for the children, their parents, and the demands of the community. Such an atmosphere dispels mistrust. In consequence the children's responses were much more reflective of their full potential, as the results showed.

REFERENCES

1. Dewey J: Human Nature and Conduct. New York, Modern Library, 1922
2. Randazzo JD, Arnold JM: Does an open education really work in an urban setting? Phi Delta Kappan 53:107–110, 1972
3. Rogers VR: Open education in Hartford: Exciting, significant, underrated. Phi Delta Kappan 53:110, 1972
4. Marianne Frostig Center of Educational Therapy: Demonstration Project in Early Childhood Education, Compton City School District, spring semester 1970. Project 75-EIA, Los Angeles, the Center, 1970
5. Frostig M: Movement Education: Theory and Practice. Chicago, Follett, 1970
6. Boehm A: The Boehm Test of Basic Concepts. New York, The Psychological Corporation, 1969
7. Frostig M, Horne D, Miller A: Pictures and Patterns: Teacher's Guides and Workbooks (rev ed). Chicago, Follett, 1972

Appendix

SAMPLE LESSON PLANS
FOR THE COMPTON PILOT PROGRAM
IN EARLY CHILDHOOD EDUCATION

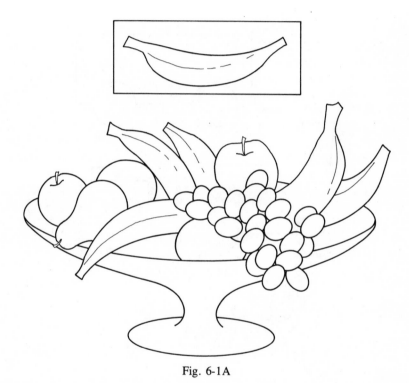

Fig. 6-1A

Fig. 6-1A,B,C.   Modified from: Frostig M, Horne D, Miller A: Beginning Pictures and Patterns (rev ed). Chicago, Follett, 1972.

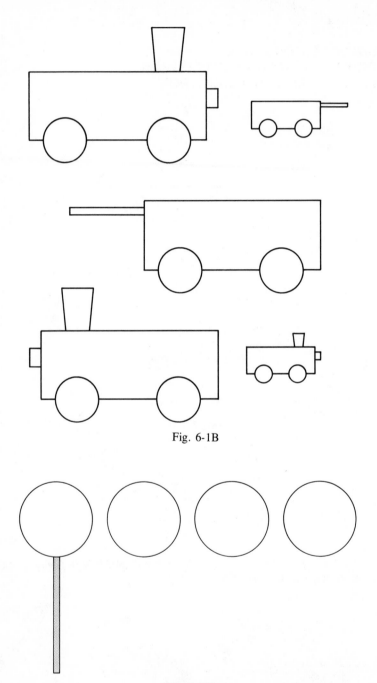

Fig. 6-1B

Fig. 6-1C

Lesson One

Materials	Teacher's Directions	Child's Desired Response	Some Learning Skills Required
1. Regular classroom furniture	"Stand *beside* your chair" *(behind, on top of, in front of)*. "Crawl *under* the table."	Appropriate physical movement.	Learning spatial concepts, associate verbal input with motor response, perception of spatial relationships. (Review; also physical activity helps to "warm up" children.)
2. Same as (1)	"Where are you?" "I am beside my chair," "I am behind my chair," and so on.	Correct verbal statements.	Verbal expression (use of complete sentences, use of spatial concepts, appropriate response to "where" questions), awareness of location of body. (Review.)
3. Circle drawn on floor with chalk	"Step *inside* this circle." "Step *outside* this circle."	Appropriate physical movement.	Learning spatial concepts, associating verbal input with motor response, perception of spatial relationships. (Review.)
4. None	"Take two steps to the *left;*" (to the *right, forward, backward*).	Appropriate physical movement.	Learning spatial concepts, associating verbal input with motor response, perception of position in space. (Review).
5. Paper and pencil	"Draw from my directions: Draw a circle. Put a square on top. Put a triangle underneath." (Child is to draw each figure before next direction is given.)	Correct drawing of figures in proper relationship.	Associating motor response with verbal input, knowledge of geometric forms, visualization, motor planning, understanding spatial concepts, eye-motor coordination. (Review.)

Lesson One, *continued*

Materials	Teacher's Directions	Child's Desired Response	Some Learning Skills Required
6. None	"Arms crossed behind. Arms to side. Arms to front. Wave them around." (Verbal directions given while teacher performs herself.)	Appropriate physical movement.	Perception of position in space, body awareness, learning of spatial concepts, learning by imitation. (Review; also a relaxing exercise, to precede a more academic section of the lesson.)
7. Plasticene or clay	"Make an M with your clay; a C; an A." (Children encouraged to say sound softly while working).	Appropriate physical and auditory movements.	Haptic perception of letter forms, multisensory perception of letter (auditory, visual, haptic), visualization, motor planning. (Review.)
8. Pictures of common objects or animals, such as monkey, man, cat, cap, apple	"Tell me what letter begins the word . . ." (as pictures are held before the class).	Correct naming of letter.	Associating visual input with verbal responses, auditory imagery (auding), visual reception, auditory analysis of word.
9. Felt letters of M, C, and A (number sufficient for half the class)	"Children, you are to work in pairs. One of you is to close your eyes, feel the felt letter, and try to tell what it is. The other member of your pair will be the teacher. Then the first one should be the teacher."	Correct naming of letter.	Haptic perception of letter forms (particularly helpful for children with inadequate visual perception), visualization, social cooperation.

10. Overhead projector transparency of intersecting letters	One child is asked to come to the projector and to outline the M in red; another child, the A in green; and so on.	Outlining the correct letter.	Visual figure-ground perception, eye-motor coordination.
11. Large cut-out letters hidden in classroom	"Find the big letters in the room. When you find one, bring it to the middle of the room and tell everyone what it is."	Finding the letter and naming it correctly.	Visual figure-ground perception, haptic perception of letter forms. (Note the degree of overlearning of these three letters, which had been introduced previously.) (This group physical activity helps lower tension and provides a transition to a new group of activities.)
12. Overhead projector transparency of Frostig Beginning Worksheet 51—see Fig. 6-1. (Emphasis of worksheet: figure-ground perception).	"What is this?" "What is this?" "What are these?" And so on.	"This is a banana." "This is an apple." "These are grapes."	Visual reception, visual-vocal integration, information in complete sentences, attention to pictorial details, visual closure (parts of the fruit are not outlined), visual figure-ground perception.
13. Bowl of plastic fruit similar to Fig. 6-1A	*To one child:* "Match this fruit with *the pear* in picture" (and so on—name the fruit).	Correct matching.	Visual reception (many children cannot associate two-dimensional pictures with their three-dimensional equivalents), visual figure-ground perception.

Lesson One, *continued*

Materials	Teacher's Directions	Child's Desired Response	Some Learning Skills Required
14. Plastic apple. Cards with letters lined against chalkboard	"Apple. What sound does it begin with? What letter makes that sound? Pick out the card with that letter."	Correct sound. Correct choice of letter.	Associating letter form and sound (auditory-visual perception), auditory analysis of word, visual figure-ground perception.
15. Plastic banana	"Imagine this is real and you are going to eat it. What would you do first? . . . Yes, peel it. . . . Can you show me how you would do that?"	Pretends to peel it.	Visualization, manual expression, motor planning.
16. Plastic banana. Cards with letters lined against chalkboard	"The banana tastes good - m-m-m. What card says that?"	Correct choice of letter.	Associating letter sound and form (auditory-visual integration), visual figure-ground perception.
17. Worksheet for each child	"Find all the bananas in the picture and outline them."	Outlines all bananas correctly.	Visual figure-ground perception, eye-motor coordination, visual closure, scanning.

76

18. Same as (17)	"How many bananas are there in the bowl? Write the number on your paper."	Writes the correct number.	Counting, writing numerals, eye-motor coordination, visual figure-ground perception. (If child makes a wrong choice—e.g., *six* bananas—he should be asked to justify it. This will help him to pay attention to details and to verbalize perceptions.)
19. Same as (17)	"What are all these called?"	"These are fruit."	Concept formation—positive instances
20. None	"Can you tell me other things that are fruit?"	Names other fruits.	Visualization, flexibility (is not bound by immediate perceptions).
21. None	"Is *cake* a fruit?"	"No."	Concept formation (negative instance), similarities and differences.
22. None	"Without looking at your picture, what fruits were in the bowl?"	Names them correctly.	Memory visualization.
23. None	"Say these in the same order: banana, apple, orange, grape." (Children sing a short song before the lesson ends.)	Repeats sequence correctly.	Auditory sequencing.

Lesson Two

Materials	Teacher's Directions	Child's Desired Response	Some Learning Skills Required
1. Cardboard cutouts of circle, triangle, square, oval, rectangle	"Name these shapes."	Names them correctly.	Perception of form constancy, visual–vocal integration. (Review.)
2. Worksheet for each child (Frostig Beginning Worksheet 53—see Fig. 6-1B. (Emphasis of worksheet: size perception.)	"What are these?"	"These are wagons." "These are engines."	Visual reception, visual-vocal integration using complete sentences.
3. Same as (2)	"What are they made of?"	"Wood." "Metal."	Identifying the attribute of "material" in manufactured products—concept formation.
4. Same as (2).	"Find all the big engines and the big wagons." "Find all the small engines and the small wagons."	Points to correct objects.	Perception of size constancy, learning quantitative concepts.
5. Classroom furnishings	"Show me a small book and a big book." "Show me a big chair and a small chair." "Find one big thing in the room; find one small thing."	Indicates correct ones.	Learning of quantitative concepts. (Concepts of "big" and "small" are applied to many different things; that helps the child to recognize that "big" and "small" are not associated with particular objects in a particular context.)

6. Pencil and paper.	"Draw a big man and a small man."	Draws figures of correct size.	Expressing instances of quantitative concepts, eye-motor coordination, body concept, body image, emotional development.
7. None	"Tell me a small number and a big number."	Replies correctly.	Seriation, counting, quantitative relationships. (This transfers concept from physical attribute to attribute of numerosity).
8. None	"Make yourelf big." "Make yourself small."	Movements interpretable as expressing the concept.	Visualization, divergent thinking, manual expression.
9. None	"Guess whether your neighbor is making himself big or small."	Indicates correctly.	Visual reception, social cooperation, manual expression.
10. None	Draw a big *A* in the air" (*M,C*). Draw a small *a* in the air" (*m,c*).	Makes correct movements.	Expressing instances of quantitative concepts, visualization, haptic perception. (This activity transfers quantitative concept to symbols and helps child conceive of letters as *arbitrary symbols*.)

(Listening to a story record ends the lesson.)

Lesson Three

Materials	Teacher's Directions	Child's Desired Response	Some Learning Skills Required
1. Transparency of Frostig Beginning Worksheet 58—See Fig. 6-1C. Lollipop for each child. (Emphasis of worksheet: eye-motor coordination)	When transparency shown: "What's missing on the lollipops?" "Where should they be?"	"The sticks are missing." "The sticks are below the circles."	Visual reception, picture completion, visual analysis, spatial relationships.
2. Worksheet of Fig. 6-1C for each child.	"Show with your fingers, then with crayon, how to draw the sticks."	Draws straight sticks in correct position.	Eye-hand coordination.
3. None	"Tell me something about lollipops."	"They are round." "We eat them." And so on.	Verbal expression; recognition that the same object has different qualities and that it can be classified differently. (*Note:* the real lollipops make this easier for children who have difficulty with language expression; they also, of course, help associate learning with pleasure.)
4. None	"What else do we eat?" After children give several examples, the teacher says: "These are all foods."	Gives verbal examples.	Visualization; classifying.

	Materials	Instruction	Behavior	Skills
5.	Cut-out paper kites, paste, paper, crayons for each child.	"Let's make a kite and put a pretty tail on it."	The kite is pasted on the paper. The tail is drawn at the bottom corner of the kite.	Eye-hand coordination
6.	None	"Tell me three things you eat and one thing you would never eat."	Responds correctly.	Ability to shift set.
7.	None	"Tell your neighbor what you had for dinner."	Communicates to neighbor.	Verbal expression, language as means of communication, social development, memory, visualization.
8.	None	"Repeat and complete these sentences for your neighbor: Yesterday I had ---- for dinner." "Tomorrow I will have ---- for dinner." "Yesterday I was in school." "Today I am in school."	Repeats sentences correctly.	Verbal expression, grammar (tense forms).
9.	None	Ask each child: "What did you do in school yesterday?" "What will you do tomorrow?" "What are you doing now?"	Answers grammatically and relevantly.	Verbal expression, visualization, planning, memory, temporal sequences, grammar (tense forms). (The children are first asked to imitate correct forms, then to use them in social communication. Ending the lesson with shared experiences helps to foster a feeling of shared interest.)

(A game of musical chairs ends the lesson.)

PART III

Evaluation and Individualized Programing of the Child with Special Educational Needs

Introduction

Intelligence is the aggregate or global capacity of the individual to act purposefully, to think rationally, and to deal effectively with his environment.

David Wechsler [1, p 3]

There is hardly a classroom anywhere in which some children do not keep pace with the majority of the class and in which many do not develop optimally, regardless of what "group" they are a member. Individualization, therefore, is an indispensable principle in teaching. It is a necessary consequence of respect for the individuality of the child and for development of each individual as a human being and as a mature member of a group. Consequently, within the structure of any program, it is necessary to ensure that each child feels comfortable in the school environment and that each one's abilities are optimally furthered. Whenever a child feels inferior, unliked, or unsuccessful, it is not only this child who is harmed, but also the other children in the classroom, who may experience anxiety, lose trust in the teacher, and defend themselves against their own anxiety by becoming hostile toward the failing child. In responding to the needs of a child in difficulty, the teacher both avoids these problems and provides the children with an example of a caring attitude. The teacher's obligation, therefore, is moral as much as educational.

Unfortunately, educators often consider it sufficient to adapt to the child's particular capabilities the level of difficulty of the tasks, the speed of progress, and the amount the child is expected to learn without change in the general program and teaching methods. Such measures are certainly an improvement and a move toward taking into account the needs of the child, particularly when so often the main regulators of the child's learning are the prescribed curriculum and the rules of the school. Nevertheless, such adaptations are merely quantitative.

Today many school authorities (mainly of the English-speaking nations) do acknowledge that qualitative differences also have to be taken into account in educating children. The kinds of programs discussed in Part II are the result of such considerations. Enrichment programs and classes for the gifted provide other examples.

In many countries the means of meeting the problem posed by children who fail to "perform" at set minimum standards is to have them repeat the school year. This is rarely an adequate solution. It is much more productive to make a careful inventory of each child's abilities and disabilities and to use this inventory as a guide for providing individualized teaching of academic skills and subject matter and for appropriate selection of methods that will help the child adjust to the social and cultural demands of the classroom. The sequence in which basic psychological abilities develop is described in Chapter 7; this sequence can serve as a framework for evaluating children's abilities and developing a program for each based on the evaluation.

Work with children with learning difficulties has spurred the development both of tests and of observational methods for gaining knowledge of children's patterns of abilities and disabilities. In Chapter 8 the standardized tests and observational procedures described can contribute to a teacher's understanding of psychological functions and to the choice of teaching methods. The importance of training basic psychological functions, here referred to as *ability training,* is necessary to ensure optimum development for all children, but especially for those with special educational needs.

Chapter 9 is devoted to case histories that illustrate how individualized programs and techniques can be applied to meet the widely varying needs of different children. Although this chapter is written primarily with children with special educational needs in mind, it has significant implications for the education of all children. *Every* child is an individual.

REFERENCE

1. Wechsler D: The Measurement of Adult Intelligence. Baltimore, Williams & Wilkins, 1944

7
Evaluation and the Developmental Sequence

It is only through a series of careful measurements of finite elements of behavior that the whole child . . . can be understood.

Anne Bowes [1]

THE STRUCTURE OF INTELLIGENCE

The training of abilities or learning skills and the adaptation of instruction to the child's individual ability pattern are relatively new concepts. They have their origins in the many studies that show that intelligence is not a unitary function but is composed of a number of different abilities. Many of these studies will be referred to in this chapter.

Research in child development has demonstrated that the structure of intelligence changes as the child matures [2,3,4,5]. Research into aptitude-treatment interactions [6] has indicated that methods that are effective for children with certain characteristics are ineffective for children with different ability patterns. Factor analytic studies of intelligence by J. P. Guilford [7] have also contributed to the understanding of the abilities necessary for learning. Most importantly, the clinical observations made by workers the world over have clearly shown that children's learning abilities improve when children receive training adapted to their individual patterns of abilities and disabilities.

The phrase *structural analysis of intelligence* has been used to denote the exploration of specific ability patterns. The term *structure* refers to the relation of parts to each other and the whole to the total organism [2, p 40]. Thus in the

87

psychological evaluation the underlying characteristics that naive observation may not discern are probed, and an exploration is made of the relationship of these characteristics to each other and to the observed behavior. Surface characteristics may tell little about the child's underlying abilities and disabilities. For instance, the observation that a child does not know which letters stand for the sounds of the digraphs *sh* and *ch* may indicate that the child has not been acquainted with digraphs or that he or she has a defect in hearing high-frequency sounds. The mere pronouncement that John made spelling mistakes writing *ch* for *sh* and vice versa does not give any indication of how to remedy Johnny's deficiency. But the underlying cause of a surface symptom can be detected by careful observations in the classroom or by the use of a well-chosen (and assembled) test battery—or best of all by a combination of both.

THE CHOICE OF DIAGNOSTIC PROCEDURES

In an attempt to find out why educational programs that are effective with most children do not work for children with "hidden" handicaps, educators have turned to psychometric tests. Psychometric tests cannot, however, be used without a theoretical framework. The choice of tests depends, first, on how one views intelligence. Intelligence is not a unitary function but is composed of several different abilities. There is no one definition of intelligence. It varies with different scientists.

Jean Piaget suggests that intelligence denotes man's ability to adapt to his environment. Alfred Binet's concept of intelligence emphasizes thinking or problem solving. Binet [8] recognizes four functions as comprising intelligence: comprehension, invention (the ability to enumerate, describe, and interpret), direction (the ability to concentrate on a given task), and censure or self-criticism. David Wechsler operationally defines intelligence as "the aggregate or global capacity of the individual to act purposefully, to think rationally, and to deal effectively with his environment" [9, p 3]. Piaget, Binet, and Wechsler have all viewed intelligence as a multiple function that is influenced by both experience and maturation.

The choice of tests used to evaluate the elusive concept "intelligence" will depend in part on whether the tests are used primarily for diagnostic classification or for prediction.

What should be emphasized is that no *single* test suffices to evaluate the abilities that are necessary for adaptation in our complicated society. Fortunately, test batteries rather than a single test are increasingly used in schools today as the basis for remediation.

Whether intelligence can be modified is a hotly disputed issue, in spite of the successful compensatory and remedial educational programs carried on throughout the world. B. S. Bloom [10], H. M. Skeels [11] and others have demonstrated that IQ scores as measured by standardized tests change over a period of time. Factor analytic studies have shown the existence of various abilities that may fluctuate independently from the total results [7,12,13].

Drastic changes in living conditions may lead to equally drastic changes in subtest scores as well as in overall intelligence test results. A survey by the Inner London Education Authority [14] showed that the mean IQ of immigrant children who had been in England for less than two years was 76; whereas for those immigrant children who had been in England more than six years, it was 91. The IQ tests were administered when the children were about 11 years of age. "We must give up the notion of intelligence as some mysterious power or faculty of the mind which everyone, regardless of race or culture, possesses in varying amounts and which determines his potentiality for achievement" [14, p 213].

Intelligence tests, it is true, are good predictors of a child's score on school achievement tests.* The scores of the latter influence, if not determine, the child's further schooling—his academic "streaming" or "tracking" and thus his career and future life status. If an educator wants to improve the child's school learning so that he will have a better chance in life, intelligence tests that result in a single score offer no assistance. Binet, who constructed the first standardized intelligence test to predict the school achievement of Parisian children, was himself strongly opposed to the notion of a unitary, unchangeable nature of intelligence:

A few philosophers seem recently to have given their moral support to these deplorable verdicts in affirming that the intelligence of an individual is a fixed quantity, a quantity which is unable to be augmented. We must protest and react against this brutal pessimism. We are going to try to demonstrate that it has no basis. [8, p 141]

As the author has stated before,

It is clear Binet regards the issue ultimately as a moral one. He is asserting a belief in the intellectual potential of the individual, and a conviction that educators have a moral obligation to help the child reach his potential. [15, p 153]

How is that obligation to be met? In order to apply specific training methods to help a child to maximize his or her intellectual abilities, we must

*Group intelligence tests are not good indicators of a child's cognitive abilities. Scores on group tests are highly influenced by motivational factors, especially self-confidence, and whether the child is "test wise"; that is, whether or not he can follow directions on computer-graded answer sheets, whether or not he knows when to guess, and so on.

first identify the specific abilities in which the child is lacking by using a well-chosen test battery. But how should this battery be chosen? Piaget has pointed out that children pass through qualitatively distinct stages. At each stage the structure of their psychological characteristics varies. The test data and observations, therefore, must be compared with the standard achievements for the child's age level.

THE DEVELOPMENTAL SEQUENCE

It is common knowledge that the ways in which a child reacts to and masters the environment change as the child grows older. The changes that occur in the growing child are evident in all aspects of development. The literature on this subject is voluminous. Most authors agree that definite sequences can be observed. The psychological functions that are necessary for all interactions with the environment and that develop according to a fixed pattern, therefore, can be called "developmental functions." (The terms "psychological functions," "basic abilities," and "learning skills" are here used interchangeably.)

As Table 7-1 shows, four groups of cognitive developmental functions are differentiated by the author—sensorimotor functions, language, perceptual skills, and higher cognitive processes. These functions develop in the same sequence in all children, although the age levels at which specific changes take place may vary somewhat from child to child or from culture to culture.

This chart shows that stages in the child's development are evident, although the stages may be defined and labeled differently by authorities. The arrows indicate that the development of an ability is not restricted to any given period; the age levels only indicate the period of *maximal* development. The "V" on the arrows indicate that all that has been learned previously is a necessary precondition for any new development and also that no new development begins suddenly, but always with an introductory period. The "V" at the bottom of each arrow indicates that development of the ability or characteristic continues, though at a slower pace than at the period of maximum development. The developmental sequence can provide the framework for defining broad areas of abilities that are necessary for a child in order to function optimally in regard to school learning. It must be remembered, however, that although different abilities develop *maximally* at different times, many aspects of development take place simultaneously.

Sensorimotor Phase

Jean Piaget [4] calls the first phase of a child's life from birth to about 18 months the sensorimotor phase; and Jerome Bruner [16] calls it the "enactive

Table 7-1

Developmental Sequence

Approx. Age	Erikson	Piaget	Freud	Frostig	Bruner
0–2 Years	Sense of Basic Trust	Sensorimotor Phase	Oral Phase	Sensorimotor Phase	Enactive
			Anal Phase		
2–4 Years	Sense of Autonomy	Preconceptual Phase	Phallic Phase	Language Phase	
4–6½ (7) Years	Sense of Initiative	Intuitive Thought	Oedipal Phase	Perceptual Phase	Ikonic
7–11 Years	Sense of Industry	Concrete Operations	Latency Period	Higher Cognitive Functions	Symbolic
11–15 Years	Sense of Identity	Formal Operations	Puberty & Adolescence		
Young Adulthood	Sense of Intimacy				
Adulthood	Sense of Generativity				
Mature Age	Ego Integrity				

period.'' During these first 18 months the child learns to orient himself in the world. Movement and sensory stimulation are combined in his first exploration of the objects with which he comes in contact.

Although any separation of skills is artificial, for practical purposes it is helpful to differentiate between the four main groups that the child acquires during this period: (1) awareness of the environment, (2) awareness of self as being separate from the environment, (3) ability to move in space, and (4) the ability to manipulate objects.

Problem solving begins with the first reactions of the child to objects in space. The desire to touch or grasp an object poses a problem for an infant. In solving the problem by employing body movement, the infant relates to the immediate environment and practices motor skills. Each newly acquired skill is extended to new objects. The child might learn, for instance, how to grasp a blanket, then a cup, then his own hand. The new skill is also adapted to different situations and modified. The child learns to grasp with either the fingers or with the whole hand, depending on the shape of the object; he adjusts his grasp so that he can get the best hold. He learns to associate various movements with various sensory inputs—for example, he sees a rattle and moves appropriately first to get it and then to shake it. Integration of movement and sensory input into a single act is the infant's most important achievement during the sensorimotor phase. Piaget terms it the "formation of a schema," and the *automatic* movements, which are the motor side of the schema, are called "habits."

Movement is the main tool in the child's interaction with the environment during infancy, a tool used for both learning and play.

The Phase of Maximum Language Development

During the second stage of development, which lasts from approximately 18 months to 2 years to about 3½ or 4 years of age, language develops maximally. A child learns to express what happens in the present and also to refer to past and future events. He can talk about things that are both accessible to his senses and absent from them. He acquires rules of syntax and builds a vast vocabulary.

Language, like the earlier developing sensorimotor functions, is a necessary building block of the intellect as well as a tool of communication. Language represents the child's observations and experiences.

The development of expressive language is the most evident achievement of this period, but it is not the only important one. At the same time two other functions—imagery and deferred imitation—develop that represent the environment to the child and help him to deal with all that is not directly evident to his senses. The child may imitate something that he has seen some time ago or talk about it and thus indicate that he can reproduce a former event. He will also listen eagerly to stories about events that he has never seen, showing that he can represent to himself the events that he hears about.

Perceptual Phase

During the next phase, which lasts from about 3½ or 4 years to about 7 years of age, the child learns many perceptual tasks. He uses the distance receptors—vision and hearing—more and more and becomes increasingly independent of the sense of touch in recognizing the attributes of objects. The child learns to differentiate between sounds in sequences, such as words; he learns to perceive the order in which he hears these sounds; he learns to perceive visually finer differences among forms in two-dimensional space and the direction of shapes on a page; he learns to interpret more complicated pictures;

he perfects the previously rudimentary ability to isolate figures from their background; he learns to perceive the order in which figures are presented; and he acquires many other visual and auditory perceptual skills. By using his eyes only, he becomes increasingly able to recognize the texture of materials, their roughness or smoothness, the evenness or unevenness of their surfaces. His hearing can tell him what vehicle passed by the window—a car, a bus, or the garbage truck.

Visual and auditory perception develop gradually, and it cannot be emphasized too strongly that the development results from the interaction of endowment and experience. For instance, the young child is unaware of perspective and has to *learn* to "understand" the spatial relationships portrayed in pictures. In a recent study it was found that many American Indian children of the Navajo tribe living in poverty in towns have difficulty in accomplishing the tasks set by the Frostig Developmental Test of Visual Perception and the Frostig perceptual training program [17]. However, Navajo children living on the reservation, where they could observe their fathers making designs in silver or with colored sand and watch their mothers weaving rugs, learned to perceive well geometrical shapes and the spatial relationships of the various parts of patterns. These children performed excellently on the relevant subtest areas of the test and program.

Piaget [4, 5] combines the stages of maximal language and perceptual development into what he calls the "preoperational stage." In turn, he divides this stage into (1) the "representational phase" (approximately 2–4 years of age) during which the child learns to use representative functions—symbolic play, deferred imitation, imagery, and language—for things and objects not immediately present to his senses and (2) the "intuitive phase" (approximately 4–7 years of age), during which the child recognizes objects immediately through visual and auditory perception without relying on movement or touch.

During the latter part of the preoperational stage (from about 4½ to 6½ years) the child not only learns many new perceptual skills, he also learns to control and regulate his actions by using the functions acquired previously, language and imagery [18].

Language and imagery may be called "mediators"; that is, they provide links between a child's perception of a stimulus and his response to it. Tracy Kendler states that "the development of the mediational process is intimately related to the development of the ability to relate words to actions" [19, p 41]. L. S. Vygotsky [20] traces the child's increasing ability to control behavior to the ability to use inner, or covert, language.

Integrational and Associative Abilities

During the latter part of the preoperational stage the child's ability to integrate the perceptions of the various senses develops maximally. People and animals do not perceive the world through vision, hearing, or touch alone. Although we are unaware of the process, our brains are normally engaged in an incessant process of integrating the stimuli that impinge on our central nervous system from our various senses. This is an essential process in our adjustment to the environment; observation of brain-damaged children and adults reveals that their frequent inability to adjust to the environment is because their perceptions of it are splintered and separated, giving only an equally splintered and separated representation.

Although infants appear able to equate stimuli from various modalities (for example, a baby may reach out his arms or make sucking movements when he hears his mother's footsteps or sees her face or smells her perfume), maximal development of integrative and associative abilities requires representational or mediational skills (language or imagery) and memory and is, therefore, a task of the later preoperational phase.* A child who is asked to execute a series of commands, for instance, must not only associate movements with auditory stimuli, he must also remember what has been said and the correct sequence of instructions.

Some children cannot carry out instructions in spite of good memory functions; they may be able to repeat the directions verbatim but still be unable to follow them. Such behavior is not uncommon in preschool children and in children with learning difficulties [24, 25]. It is considered to result from the child's inability to imagine the desired results (mentally produce an image or model). The integrative functions of some children can be improved by having them perform tasks in sequences of small steps, first with the teacher simultaneously verbalizing what they are doing, then with their own verbalization or diagraming of the sequence, and then with the children closing their eyes and "picturing" what happens after each step. The children use language and imagery consciously in this way until they are able to mediate automatically.

Children have to learn to integrate stimuli received from either the same or from two or more sense channels simultaneously, to associate perceptions and responses, and to remember (to associate present perceptions with representations of previous ones). They also have to learn to react selectively to simultaneous stimuli. For instance, an automobile driver may be receiving simul-

---

*Cross-modal learning as investigated by H. G. Birch and A. Lefford [21] requires the child to pay attention to and to remember abstract stimuli. Children below 5 years of age were usually not able to equate an abstract pattern presented auditorily with one presented visually, or vice versa. It is interesting to note that the Kendlers [18] found maximal development of mediational skills occurring after about 5 years of age and that G. Ettinger [22] ascribes deficits in integrational abilities to lack of verbal mediation. S. A. Rose, M. S. Blank, and W. H. Bridger [23] believe difficulties in cross-modal integration are due primarily to difficulties in memory. To assist children in the acquisition of mediational skills, specific exercises should be used to stimulate verbal mediation, memory skills, and imagery.

taneous signals from the road in front of him, the driver behind him (as viewed in his rear-view mirror), the car radio, and the remarks of his friend. If he is to arrive safely at his destination, he must attend to each appropriately and be able to "tune out" and "tune in" selectively. Thus, if he hears a fire-truck siren, he must be able to switch his attention to it, pull off to the side of the road, and only later resume his conversation with his friend.

The Phase of Higher Cognitive Functions

In the author's developmental sequence the last "distinct" stage of development begins at about 7 years of age and continues on into adulthood. This is the phase of higher cognitive functions. Piaget, however, denotes two stages for this phase of development—the concrete operational phase (approximately 7 to 11 years of age) and the formal operational phase (approximately 11 to 15 years of age).

During the period from about 6½ or 7 to about 11 years of age conceptual thinking is developing rapidly. It builds strongly on the preceding phase. Concepts develop on the basis of perceptual experiences. Percepts stand not only for individual objects, such as a particular table, but they also stand for the concept of which the immediate percept is an example: for example, a piece of furniture with a flat top on which objects may be placed is a "table." George Berkeley stated, "An idea which considered in itself is particular, becomes general by being made to represent or stand for all other particular ideas of the same sort" [26, p 155]. Perception itself always presupposes categorization. When we recognize something as a table, a square, or a plant, it means that we have grouped these particular objects into the categories of tables, squares, and plants.

It is due to previously learned skills that the child can now learn to classify not only perceptually, for instance, by color or form, but also to use functional and abstract and hierarchical relationships. He will learn to shift the basis of classification. A wool blanket, for instance, can be conceived as a member of a class of material things, a thing made of organic material, made from animal products, made from products of domesticated animals. It is also a woven product, a textile, a colored product. It is pliable, soft, warm, and inflammable. It is something used as a cover, as clothing, for riding, for sleeping, for transporting people after accidents. It is an object that gives security to infants and young children and serves as a *table d'hote* for moth larvae.

In paying attention first to one attribute and then to another one of the same object, the child begins to make multiple classifications and to understand ways in which two objects are the same, similar, and different.

The child can now use thought processes to check perceptions. For instance, if a child who has entered the stage of concrete operations sees two balls of clay the same size and then one ball is rolled out in a long snakelike form, this child is able to state that both the ball and the "snake" consist of the same amount of clay because he is able to imagine the snake being rolled back into a ball (which illustrates an operation called "reversibility"). He also realizes that though the "snake" is longer, it is also thinner (which illustrates the child's ability to consider the relationship of two or more attributes simultaneously), and he recognizes that no substance has been added or taken away.

These new cognitive skills, however, would be impossible without the skills achieved earlier. The close connection between imagery and thought is paralleled by the close connection between perception and concept formation. Rudolf Arnheim states,

> My contention is that the cognitive operations called thinking are not the privilege of mental processes above and beyond perception, but the essential ingredients of perception itself. I am referring to such operations as active exploration, selection, grasping of essentials, simplification, abstraction, analysis and synthesis, completion, correction, comparison, problem solving, as well as combining, separating, putting in context. By "cognitive" I mean all mental operations involved in the receiving, storing, and processing of information: sensory perception, thinking, learning [26, p 3].

He adds,

> In the perception of shape lie the beginnings of concept formation. . . . What matters is that an object at which someone is looking can be said to be truly perceived to the extent to which it is fitted to some organized shape [26, p 27].

At about 12 to 13 years of age children become able to think logically without referring to things actually perceived. They can now formulate and evaluate scientific hypotheses. They can understand the laws of probability and abstract mathematics and symbolic logic. Piaget refers to the stage in which these and other similar abilities belong as the stage of formal operations. Since this book deals mainly with the problems of the elementary school child, this stage will not be discussed in greater detail.

EMOTIONAL AND SOCIAL DEVELOPMENT

The functions that have been discussed—sensorimotor abilities, language, perception, and higher cognitive processes—and the integration of these abilities make it possible to understand, to know, and to communicate with the environment. While these abilities develop maximally at certain age levels, there are two other groups of psychological functions that do not develop maximally at a specific time—emotional development and social development. They develop throughout life, taking various forms depending on the circumstances and the main role of the human being during the various phases of his life. As is emphasized throughout the book, these are of major importance because they influence all other aspects of the child's development, including the process of learning and ethical and moral development. The significance of these facts is recognized even by teachers who regard the child's cognitive development as their only responsibility.

The teacher should, therefore, take note of behavior that suggests emotional problems or social immaturity. Is a child frequently sad or angry? Does Mary tease a great deal or seem to be always in fights or arguments? Is Tom particularly quiet, withdrawn, and unassertive? (Often difficulties that such a child might have are ignored because the behavior does not cause disturbance in the classroom.) Is Robert a loner and always apart from the group? Is he the scapegoat for other children? Does he tend not to participate in the classroom and playyard activities? Does Amy give up easily if a task is difficult for her? Is she unable to tolerate making mistakes? Does Tommy overreact to minor physical hurts or teasing or aggressiveness on the part of another child? Does he cling to the teacher? Or is he very "bossy"?

The teacher should always be aware that any of these manifestations may be related to disabilities in the developmental skills discussed earlier and thus reflect the child's consequent insecurity, former experiences of failure, fragmented perceptions, and difficulty in perceiving social situations or the feelings or intentions of others accurately. They may also reflect situations in the home or in the child's upbringing that provoke anxiety or retard maturity. Whatever the cause, they are likely to affect the child's ability to learn to the best of his or her capabilities, and will certainly adversely influence overall development. These behaviors, therefore, need to be taken into account by the teacher and responded to appropriately.

REFERENCES

1. Bowes A: Position paper for a workshop on perceptual motor dysfunction, presented at a meeting of the American Orthopsychiatric Association, San Francisco, 1966
2. Gardner H: The Quest for Mind: Piaget, Levi-Strauss, and the Structuralist Movement. New York, Knopf, 1973
3. Piaget J: The Construction of Reality in the Child. New York, Basic Books, 1954
4. Piaget J: The Origins of Intelligence in Children (ed 2). New York, Norton, 1963
5. Piaget J, Inhelder B: The Psychology of the Child. New York, Basic Books, 1969

6. Cronbach LJ, Snow RE: Individual Differences in Learning Ability as a Function of Instructional Variables. Washington, D.C., U.S. Office of Education, March 1969. ERIC No.029-001
7. Guilford JP: The Nature of Human Intelligence. New York, McGraw-Hill, 1967
8. Binet A. Les idees modernes sur les enfants. Paris, Flammarion, 1909
9. Wechsler D: The Measurement of Adult Intelligence. Baltimore, Williams & Wilkins, 1944
10. Bloom BS: Stability and Change in Human Characteristics. New York, Wiley, 1964
11. Skeels HM: Adult Status of Children with Contrasting Early Life Experiences. Monographs of the Society for Research in Child Development 31(3, Whole No. 105), 1966
12. Thurstone LL, Thurstone TG: Factorial Studies of Intelligence. Psychometric Monographs (2). Chicago, University of Chicago, 1941
13. Vernon PE: Intelligence and Cultural Environment. London, Metheun, 1969
14. Inner London Education Authority: The Education of Immigrant Pupils in Primary Schools. ILEA Report No. 959. London, Her Majesty's Stationery Office, 1967
15. Frostig M: The analysis of cognitive and communicative abilities. J Spec Ed 5:151–153, 1971
16. Bruner JS, et al: Studies in Cognitive Growth, New York, Wiley, 1966
17. Dennis DM, Dennis MN: A Study of Visual Perception in Early Childhood. Washington, D.C., U.S. Office of Education, 1968. ERIC No.023-451
18. Kendler TS, Kendler HH: Reversal and nonreversal shifts in kindergarten children. J Exp Psychol 58:59–60, 1959
19. Kendler TS: Development of mediating responses in children, in Wright JC, Kagan J (eds): Basic Cognitive Processes in Children. Monographs of the Society for Research in Child Development 28(2, Serial No. 86), 1963
20. Vygotsky LS: Thought and Language. Cambridge, Mass., MIT Press, 1962
21. Birch HG, Lefford A: Visual Differentiation, Intersensory Integration, and Voluntary Motor Control. Monographs of the Society for Research in Child Development 32(2, Serial No. 110), 1967
22. Ettinger G: Analysis of cross-modal effects and their relationship to language, in Darley FL, Millikan CH (eds): Brain Mechanisms Underlying Speech and Language. New York, Grune & Stratton, 1967
23. Rose SA, Blank MS, Bridger WH: Intermodal and intramodal retention of visual and factual information in young children. Dev Psychol 6(3):482–486, 1972
24. Farnham-Diggory S: Cognitive Synthesis in Negro and White Children. Monographs of the Society for Research in Child Development 35(2, Serial No. 135), 1970
25. Bem SL: The role of comprehension in children's problem-solving. Dev. Psychol 2(3):351–358, 1970
26. Arnheim R: Visual Thinking. Berkeley, University of California Press, 1969

8
Assessment of Basic Abilities

There does remain some structure in the way we can separate, describe, and measure these functions employed by humans engaging in productive intellectual activity. The application *of our intelligence depends upon the growth of these functions [abilities]. In teaching children to learn, this structure provides us with a relatively secure base upon which we can fashion learning experiences.*

Mary Meeker [1, p 6]

We have already noted that numerous standardized tests are available to assess a child's abilities in the major developmental functions relative to those of agemates in sensorimotor abilities, language, auditory and visual perception, and higher cognitive processes. Familiarity with at least one or two tests in each of these areas will enable the teacher to assist the child more effectively in acquiring these needed skills. Even though the teacher may never administer the tests, knowledge of what the tests are designed to measure will facilitate the understanding of each child's functioning, will produce better informal assessments of the child's pattern of abilities and disabilities, and, when the test results are available, will enable the teacher to use them more adequately as the basis for individual programing.

Sometimes standardized test results are not available. However, if the teacher knows what behaviors are tapped by psychometric tests, it is possible to observe in the classroom and on the playground the behaviors that reflect a child's developmental abilities and make comparisons with agemates' behaviors in order to arrive at a rough assessment of the child's capabilities. For more precise information, the teacher can ask the child to perform certain tasks that require the abilities to be assessed—in other words, the teacher can give informal tests. This is simply an extension of the teacher's normal practice of constructing tests to check on the child's acquisition of *academic* skills and content.*

The importance of observation is not restricted to those occasions when information is needed and test results are unavailable. Ongoing observation is always needed to supplement ratings from screening tests and scores from test batteries. Any test, formal or informal, samples only a limited number of a child's behaviors at one point in time. A child may be able to perform well on a test when he can concentrate on "one thing" for a short period of time, but the same child may be unable to perform adequately a number of similar tasks during the day. The reverse situation may also be true; a child may be ill or tired when tested, or he may dislike the examiner, or some other situational circumstance may affect the child's test performance so that it does not give a true indication of his ability. The teacher, therefore, must be involved in a process of continual evaluation. This is also essential because a teacher must always be able to determine how effective a child's educational program is proving and have the necessary information to be able to make specific adaptations accordingly. An effective program has to be based on careful, continuing systematic observation and informal testing as well as on more formal testing and retesting, whenever this is available.

This chapter includes a description of a test battery. At the end of the description of each subtest of that battery suggestions are made for appropriate tasks that can substitute for or augment the subtest results.

SCREENING TESTS

It is particularly important for the teacher to check the child's level of development in various abilities at the age of school entry (kindergarten or first grade). Screening tests have been developed in many countries for this purpose. A Teacher's School Entry Screening Test, developed by Marlene Sheppard [2], is used widely in Australia and to a lesser degree in the United States and England. Other examples of good screening tests include the evaluative instruments used by the National Children's Bureau in the United Kingdom in their National Child Development Study. In the United States there are a great many instruments available that effectively achieve their goal of assessment of a child's abilities.

Screening and readiness tests are being used increasingly in the United States. They usually include the same groups of abilities as tested with the test

---

*If a child's behavior and performance seems markedly deviant from that of agemates and if the teacher's best efforts in individualized programing do not seem to help the child in the course of several months, every effort should be made to have the child evaluated intensively and comprehensively by a professional consultant, if possible by a multidisciplinary team.

battery to be described in this volume. Examples are those by K. de Hirsch, J. Jansky, and W. Langford [3], J. Pate and W. Webb [4], and J. H. Meier, V. O. Cozier, and M. T. Giles [5]. New York City's Let's Look at Children [6] was designed to help teachers better understand, assess, and foster the intellectual development of first grade children. The Cooperative Preschool Inventory [7], developed for use with children from 3 to 6 years of age, assesses achievement in areas regarded as necessary for success in school. CIRCUS [8] is designed to assess specific perceptual-motor and cognitive-linguistic skills and characteristics in preprimary children. In addition, the CIRCUS program provides a behavior inventory that helps the teacher to rate the child's reaction to the measures tested (the degree of interest, attention, and so on).

Screening tests serve different purposes. They are of value when used to discover those children who need remediation. They are potentially damaging when used as the sole or main basis for decisions that may greatly influence children's lives, such as segregation into various special classes or postponement of school entry.

It is important to emphasize that the same caveat applies to screening devices and teacher's ratings as to test batteries—they should *never* be used for purposes of categorization. Their value is to permit the teacher to choose activities for the child more wisely and to guide the child more effectively. It is indeed unfortunate that some screening devices (not those mentioned here) encourage the application of such labels as neurologically impaired. Such labels do not help the teacher in programing for the child; rather they tend to be interpreted as predictions despite the fact that there is no other evidence for this diagnosis or that the developmental lags revealed by the test will persist. Nor does labeling specify conditions under which the lags might persist or be overcome. Screening instruments that arrive at a "label" should be only the first step in a complete assessment.

A Test Battery Designed to Assess Basic Abilities

The five standardized tests described in detail in this chapter constitute the basic test battery given by the Marianne Frostig Center of Educational Therapy to all children referred because of learning difficulties. They are the Frostig Movement Skills Test Battery [9], the Marianne Frostig Developmental Test of Visual Perception [10], the Wepman Test of Auditory Discrimination [11], the Illinois Test of Psycholinguistic Abilities (ITPA) [12], and the Wechsler Intelligence Scale for Children (WISC) [13]. To these tests others are added, depending on the needs of the child. The sensorimotor skills and the test of visual perceptual functions have been developed at the Frostig Center and standardized by the Center's psychological staff in cooperation with outside consultants. It was necessary to develop these tests since none were available that differentiated between the various sensorimotor and visual perceptual abilities assessed by the subtests.

EVALUATING SENSORIMOTOR ABILITIES

The teacher needs to be concerned with various aspects of the child's sensorimotor functions. Four groups have been mentioned: awareness of the outside world, body awareness, motor skills, and visual-motor skills and fine motor coordination.

Awareness of the Outside World

In some psychotic children awareness of the outside world is grossly disturbed and is mirrored in the child's total behavior, including the lack of interest in the outside world and the lack of knowledge and judgment of events.

Body Awareness

All skilled movement requires body awareness. In neurosis and psychosis body awareness is often disturbed, and the perception of body boundaries is fluid. Neurotic and psychotic older children, and also healthy young children, may become panicky because they feel mutilated whenever they are not in body contact with a certain object, such as a toy or blanket.

Fig. 8-1.   What a delightful feeling! Exercises on the trampoline are not only fun, but also help develop body awareness. (Photo by James Quinn and Michael Campa.)

Children's drawings reflect the representation that children have of their body, and their feelings connected with it. Therefore, these provide an excellent basis for the assessment of both the child's emotional and intellectual functions. The child's body image is affected by all of the child's experiences. It is intimately connected with self-respect and, particularly in the young child, with the feeling of being a "person" who is separate from his environment and who can influence it. The teacher's knowledge of the individual child and his or her observations will help in assessing the body awareness of each student in the classroom. For example, the teacher will need to ask: Can the child locate and identify body parts? Does he know right and left on his own body? In what sort of terms does he refer to himself (such as, "I'm big and strong!")? Is he able to "find" the parts of the body, for instance, when told to touch his neck, or his ankle, or his knee? The teacher will also gain information from the child's drawing of the human body, as already mentioned.

Assessment of Visual-Motor Skills and Attributes of Movement

The Frostig Movement Skills Test Battery [9] tests motor skills. The battery consists of twelve subtests designed to assess eye-hand coordination, balance, strength, flexibility, and visually guided movement [14].* Table 8–1 lists each subtest and notes the ability assessed.

The test battery requires about 20 minutes for administration to an individual child. A group of three or four children can be individually tested in about 40 minutes. (Time is saved in the group procedure by explaining and demonstrating each activity to the group, then having each child perform the task individually.) This test can be given and interpreted by a classroom teacher who has had *training and practice* in administering it, provided psychological consultation is available.**

Normative data are provided separately for girls and boys for seven age groups from 6 through 12 years of age. The raw scores are converted to scale scores with a mean of 10 and a standard deviation of 3. A "profile of abilities" summary sheet groups the subtests that consistently have had relatively high loadings on a particular factor (hand-eye coordination, strength, balance, visually guided movement, and flexibility).

The Move-Grow-Learn Movement Skills (M-G-L) Survey [19] was developed to assist classroom teachers and other professional personnel to observe and evaluate informally selected aspects of a child's psychomotor

---

*Examples of other motor tests are the Krauss-Weber Test [15], the Purdue Perceptual-Motor Survey [16], the Lincoln-Oseretsky Test [17], and the Cratty battery [18].

**A super-8 film or videotape demonstrating this test can be obtained from the Marianne Frostig Center for Educational Therapy, 5981 Venice Boulevard, Los Angeles, Calif. 90034.

Table 8–1

The Frostig Movement Skills Test Battery

Subtest	Ability Assessed
1. Bead stringing	Bilateral eye-hand coordination and dexterity.
2. Fist/edge/palm	Unilateral coordination involving motor sequencing.
3. Block transfer	Eye-hand and fine motor coordination involving crossing the midline of the body. (Children with learning difficulties are frequently deficient in this ability).
4. Bean-bag throw	Visual-motor coordination involving aiming and accuracy.
5. Sitting/bending/reaching	Ability to flex spine, back muscles, and hamstring ligaments.
6. Standing broad jump	Leg strength.
7. Shuttle run	Running speed and ability to make quick stops, changes of direction, and changes of body position
8. Changing body position	Speed and agility in changing body position from a lying to a standing position.
9. Sit-ups	Abdominal muscle strength.
10. Walking board	Ability to maintain dynamic balance.
11. One-foot balance:	
a. Eyes open	Static balance with eyes open.
b. Eyes closed	Static balance with eyes closed.
12. Chair push-ups	Arm and shoulder girdle muscle strength.

development. The survey is intended to be used in conjunction with the Move-Grow-Learn program [20]. Unlike the Frostig Movement Skills Test Battery, the M-G-L Survey is not a standardized psychometric instrument that provides developmental norms. It is a rating scale whereby the teacher can rate each child in relation to agemates in regard to movement skills by observation in the classroom and on the playground.

Most attributes of movement in the M-G-L Survey were identified in previous factor analytic studies of psychomotor abilities [12, 22, 23]. In addition to the motor abilities in the M-G-L Survey and their definitions, behaviors that can be easily observed by the classroom teacher to estimate the particular abilities are given in Table 8–2.

Although there are several standardized tests for various kinds of fine motor coordination, they are used primarily for vocational guidance and generally require special apparatus [24]. An indication of a child's fine motor coordination can be obtained, however, by use of the scores of the Frostig Movement Skills Test Battery. The teacher can also easily assess a child's ability to perform tasks requiring fine motor coordination by observing such self-help skills as tying shoelaces, buttoning a coat, and zipping trousers or a jacket and by comparing a child's performance with that of agemates in arts and crafts activities (such as cutting, pasting, drawing, coloring, and the like). The teacher should note particularly whether the child uses one hand consistently and whether he can cross the midline of his body (for example, can he thread a bead held in his preferred hand on a wire placed to his opposite side?).

The teacher should also observe the child's eye movements. For example, do his eyes follow smoothly a swinging pendulum or a colored knot on a slowly twirling hoop? [25, pp 22–23]

EVALUATING AUDITORY PERCEPTION

Like visual perception, auditory perception consists of a number of differentiated abilities rather than a single global entity. Auditory perceptual skills involve auditory discrimination (the ability to differentiate, for example, between *bed* and *bad*), auditory figure-ground perception (the ability to pay attention to relevant sounds and to ignore irrelevant ones, such as perceiving the umpire's call in a noisy gymnasium), auditory closure, recognition and discrimination of auditory sequences (recognizing, for example, that the *r* in bridge comes after the *b* and before the *i* and so on), memory for auditory sequences, and sound blending.

Auditory Discrimination

The most commonly used test of auditory perception, the Wepman Test of Auditory Discrimination [11], assesses auditory discrimination of whole words; it requires the child to indicate in some manner whether two words that are said to him, such as *thief* and *sheaf,* are the same or different.* The Wepman Test is quickly and easily administered and can be given by the classroom teacher if the backup support of a psychologist is available.

The teacher should check the kinds of errors made by the child in discriminating sounds and words. Not infrequently children have a high frequency hearing loss, and they do not hear clearly such phonemes as *v, ch,* or *th.* Children with this deficit should be seated in front of the teacher where they can watch the teacher's lips during instruction.

*The child's ability to understand these concepts (same, different) must be checked before the test is administered.

Table 8–2

The Move-Grow-Learn Movement Skills Survey

Motor Ability		Representative Behavior
Coordination and rhythm	Harmonious combination or interaction of motions. Rhythm denotes flowing, measured, balanced movement.	
Gross motor	Simultaneous and coordinated use of several muscles or muscle groups.	Skipping, galloping, rope jumping.
Fine motor	The ability to integrate the movements of fingers, hands, wrists into a purposeful, synchronized pattern.	Writing, cutting, color-
Eye-motor	The ability to coordinate movements of the body with vision.	Throwing at a target, avoiding collisions, hammering nails, sawing, and nearly all other activities requiring fine motor coordination.
Agility	The ability to initiate movement, change direction, or otherwise adjust position speedily.	Avoiding the ball in a game of dodgeball.
Flexibility	The ability to move parts of the body easily in relation to each other with maximum joint extension and flexion.	Touching the floor while keeping the knees straight.
Strength	The force exerted with the whole body or with parts of it.	Sit-ups (abdominal muscle strength necessary), broad jumping (leg strength) throwing objects (arm strength).
Speed	The tempo achieved during a movement sequence.	Running, racing.

Table 8–2 *(continued)*

Motor Ability		Representative Behavior
Balance	The ability to maintain a position with minimal contact with a surface.	
Static	Balance in which the surface is stable and the person is not moving.	Standing on one leg or tiptoe.
Dynamic	Maintaining a position on a moving surface or during movement.	Walking across a balance beam.
Object	Using a minimal body surface to support an object without letting it fall.	Running with a ball or other object held on the outstretched palm without letting it fall.
Endurance	The ability to sustain physical activity and resist muscular fatigue.	(Should not be rated in elementary school except when physical achievement tests given that include endurance tasks.)

Some children are able to understand complicated passages and to perceive differences between words but are unable to distinguish speech sounds in isolation. The teacher can ask the child to indicate, for instance, if $\breve{a}$ and $\breve{e}$, $\breve{\imath}$ and $\breve{u}$, $\breve{a}$ and $\breve{o}$, v and f sound the same or different. If the child can read, he can point to a word containing the sound pronounced, for example, *pat* or *pet* when *e* is pronounced.

Auditory Figure-Ground Perception

The child's auditory figure-ground perception can be checked, not only by standardized tests but also by observing how well the child can understand what is said when there is a great deal of background noise in the room. The teacher can also ask children to indicate when they hear a certain word in a story. This activity makes an enjoyable small-group game.

Auditory Closure

The auditory closure subtest of the Illinois Test of Psycholinguistic Abilities, or ITPA, requires the child to recognize words or phrases in which certain sounds have been omitted (for example, Ea.ter .unny—Easter bunny). To do this well, the child has to have an adequate vocabulary (that is, have the word or phrase in his language repertoire). In addition, he must be able to hear all the sounds in a word and to remember the sounds. A child who cannot understand telephone conversations, or the remarks of someone with an unfamiliar accent, or a radio or TV announcer when there is minor electrical interference is likely to have auditory closure difficulties.

Recognition and Discrimination of Auditory Sequences

Many children with learning difficulties cannot recognize the boundaries of a word or of a phoneme in an auditory sequence. Such a child cannot state correctly the number of separate sounds in a word or the number of words in a sentence. This disability constitutes a major obstacle to learning to read and write. In checking on this ability, the teacher can begin by having the child first reproduce a short nonverbal rhythm by clapping or stamping, then explore whether the child can state *how* many different sounds he hears in words, and finally whether he can enumerate how many words he hears in sentences said to him by the teacher. The teacher should also ask the child whether sounds in two words occur in the same or in a different order—for example, top–pot, pills––spill. Children with difficulties in the discrimination of auditory sequences are likely to confuse such words.

Memory for Auditory Sequences

The child's memory for auditory material can be assessed by the auditory sequential memory subtest of the Illinois Test of Psycholinguistic Abilities (ITPA) [12] and the digit span subtest of the Wechsler Intelligence Scale for Children (WISC) [13], although these subtests tap only short-term memory for a series of unrelated digits.

The ITPA auditory sequential memory subtest requires the child to repeat a series of digits presented rapidly. In the WISC digit span subtest the numbers are presented more slowly so that the child has an opportunity to "chunk" them, that is, to remember two or more as unit. It is easier to remember 26-78-10 than 2-6-7-8-1-0. The WISC digit span subtest also requires the child to repeat the digits in reverse order; for example, the child is given a sequence such as 5-3-7-1, and he must reply 1-7-3-5. This is called "digit span backward" and requires the child to employ mental manipulation and imagery.

Even when these subtest scores are available, the findings have to be supplemented by checking the ability to repeat a series of unconnected words and of connected phrases or sentences of varying length. The teacher can obtain an indication of a child's long-term auditory memory by observing whether the child retains such sequences as the days of the week, months of the year, telephone numbers, multiplication tables, and the like.

Sound Blending

An important ability in learning to read is sound blending. A child may be able to discriminate sounds and to remember them in the proper order yet still be unable to synthesize them into a word. The sound-blending test of the ITPA,* the Roswell-Chall Sound Blending Test [26], and a section of the Spache [27], assess this ability. The teacher's observation of the child's performance in similar beginning reading tasks (such as, *c-a-t, cat; m-a-n, man*) may serve equally well.

EVALUATING VISUAL PERCEPTUAL SKILLS

The Marianne Frostig Developmental Test of Visual Perception [10] was designed to assess a child's abilities in five subareas of visual perception that clinical observation and experience have shown are necessary for a child to progress satisfactorily in school and to adjust to environmental demands. This assessment can then serve as the basis for individualized programing. The research of L. L. Thurstone [28], K. Wedell [29], and W. M. Cruickshank and his associates [30], among others, supports the assumption that a number of visual perceptual abilities exist.

The first subtest of the Frostig test consists of tasks requiring eye-motor coordination. Eye-motor coordination can be evaluated in the classroom when watching children draw, write numerals, print, or script write. Other everyday school activities provide ample opportunity for the teacher to note eye-motor coordination.

The second subtest assesses figure-ground perception. This ability can be observed in such school-related tasks as finding a specific fact in a paragraph or

---

*In this subtest, sounds are spoken at half-second intervals (for example, *m-i-s*), and the child must reply with the word they form *(mice)*.

a word in a dictionary, index, or glossary. The third subtest taps the perception of form constancy. This skill is required for recognizing letters or words when printed in various type styles. Some children can learn to read in one series of preprimers but have difficulty in reading other preprimers with different styles of type. Poor perceptual constancy may also result in difficulty in discriminating between such similar letters as *m* and *n*.

The fourth subtest assesses perception of position in space, which is necessary for distinguishing, for example, between rotated or reversed letters and words (such as *p* and *q, b* and *d, on* and *no.*) Children who read and write *b* for *d* may have difficulties in the perception of position in space, or they may have associational defects, being able to differentiate between the directions of the letters but not able to remember which direction is associated with which letter name. The teacher can find the cause for this very simply. The child is given a sheet of paper on which identical figures are drawn, some facing one way and some the other, and is asked to say which figures are the same and which different.

The fifth and final subtest of the Frostig test explores perception of spatial relationships, an ability required for discriminating the sequence of letters in a word, for instance, or the order in which numbers are to be divided and multiplied in a long-division problem.

Table 8–3 summarizes the Frostig Developmental Test of Visual Perception and suggests activities to help children with difficulties with these visual perceptual tasks.

Other tests of visual perceptual ability are often included in the battery, including the Bender Visual Motor Gestalt Test [31] and the Goodenough Draw-A-Man Test [32]. Both tests require the child to be able to reproduce figures. The Bender Gestalt Test also draws upon motor planning, and the Goodenough involves body concept and body image among other factors. Neither test differentiates among several visual perceptual abilities as does the Frostig test, but they are useful supplements. In addition, the ITPA can be used to assess visual memory skills, using the visual sequential memory subtest. The ITPA also evaluates visual closure. Both of these skills will be discussed later.

In addition to observing the child's performance of school tasks, the teacher who does not have standardized test results available may give the class visual perceptual training exercises, such as those from *Pictures and Patterns* [25], and compare the performance of an individual child with that of agemates. The instructor should be certain to check the child's ability to discriminate and remember a visual sequence; for instance, the teacher might draw a figural sequence (▲○□▲) on the blackboard, erase it, and have the child select the one that he saw from among similar sequences (▲▲□○, ▲○○□, ▲○□▲, ○▲▲□). The teacher should also observe how well the child copies a pattern, a word, or a short sentence from the chalkboard.

EVALUATING COMMUNICATIVE SKILLS

The standardized test most frequently used to assess communicative abilities is the Illinois Test of Psycholinguistic Abilities (ITPA) [12]. It assesses not only receptive and expressive language but also the child's ability to use meaningful symbols, to process information automatically, to organize and associate perceptions and concepts, to utilize imagery, and to remember sequences. According to B. D. Bateman,

> One of the greatest contributions of the ITPA is that it has provided a frame of reference which makes it easier to know which behavior to observe, facilitates the observation, and provides guidelines for planning the modification of those behaviors through remediation [33, p 92].

The summary of the ITPA tests in Table 8–4 is a convenient reference tool for the discussion that follows.

Subtests of "Automatic" Behaviors

The ITPA subtests of visual sequential memory, auditory sequential memory, sound blending, auditory closure, and visual closure are considered by the ITPA model to be on the *automatic* level; that is, they tap behavior that is highly organized but is performed below the level of much conscious awareness [34, 35].

The grammatic closure subtest is also on the automatic level because children learn and use correct language forms in an automatic way. In this ITPA subtest the child is shown a picture, for example, of a dog. "Here is a dog." He is shown a picture of two dogs. "Here are two __." The child completes the sentence with "dogs," indicating that he understands the plural formation of regular nouns.

The observation of the child's "natural" use of language will give the teacher as accurate a determination as any standardized test. Observation will also permit appraisal of the child's articulation, an automatic function not covered by the ITPA.

Auditory Reception and Visual Reception

Two subtests of the ITPA, auditory reception and visual reception, tap the ability to recognize and understand what is heard and seen. These tests, as well as those discussed below, are subtests on the *representational* level, requiring the use of concepts and meaningful symbols. In the auditory reception subtest the child is to answer "yes" or "no" to such questions as "Do babies drink?" "Do barometers congratulate?" The child not only has to recognize and discriminate the words and to know the meaning of each word separately, but also

Table 8-3
Frostig Developmental Test of Visual Perception (Summary)

Subtest Name	Example	Some Functions Covered	Some Suggested Training Procedures
Eye-motor coordination	"Draw straight lines horizontally." "Stop and start on target."	Eye-hand coordination (necessary for handwriting, drawing, arts and crafts, manipulatory and self-help activities).	Eye movement training, arts and crafts, manipulatory exercises, handwriting exercises, physical education program.
Figure-ground	"Find a hidden figure." "Find one of two or several intersecting figures."	Ability to focus visually on relevant aspects of visual field and "tune out" irrelevant background.	"Finding" games (e.g., hidden figures included in many children's activity books), sorting exercises, unscrambling intersecting words etc.
Form constancy	"Find all the squares on a page regardless of color, background, tilt, size."	Ability to see sameness of essential form despite changes of image on retina. Has implication for learning to identify letters presented in various prints.	Identifying objects or drawing at different distances or angles, drawing diagrams of 3-dimensional patterns, finding all objects of a certain shape in the room.

112

Position in space	"Find the form that is reversed or rotated."	Ability to discriminate position, ability to differentiate letters such as *d* and *b*, *w* and *m*.	Exercises promoting awareness of body position in relation to objects (go under the table, over chair, around the desk,.etc.), physical education program, learning directions in space—right, left.
Spatial relations	"Duplicate a dot pattern by linking dots with a line."	Ability to see spatial relationships of objects to one another, related to ability to perceive the sequence of letters in a word.	Copying patterns with pegs, beads, marbles; puzzles.

From M. Frostig and P. Maslow, *Learning Problems in the Classroom* (New York, Grune & Stratton, 1973), pp. 126–127.

Table 8–4
Subtests of the Illinois Test of Psycholinguistic Abilities

	Test Description	Examples of Classroom Observations
Auditory reception	The child indicates "yes" or "no" to such questions as "Do babies drink?" "Do barometers congratulate?"	Does the child understand what is said? Can he follow written directions but not verbal ones? Can he take down dictated sentences? Can he identify common animal sounds? musical instruments? classroom noises?
Visual reception	The child must select from a group of pictures the one of an object that is used in a same or similar way as a stimulus picture.	Can the child get specific requested information from pictures or films? Does he have a wide acquantance with everyday objects, such as tools?
Manual expression	The child must show through gesture how an object (e.g., a phone, a toothbrush) is used.	Can the child express action through movement? Can the child play charades? Is he hesitant and awkward when the class does creative movement?
Verbal expression	The child is asked to describe a familiar object, such as a ball.	How well does the child express himself? How many different concepts does he use? Is he creative and imaginative?
Auditory association	The child is required to make analogies in completing sentences: e.g., "Cotton is soft; stones are [hard]."	Does the child understand the concepts of "same" and "different?" Can he understand math relationships? Does he have difficulty in classifying?
Visual association	The child must associate pictures on the basis of relationships such as functional usage (sock and shoe) and conceptual categories (horse and cow, both animals; bread and cheese, both foods).	How large is the child's store of concepts? Does he make logical connections between ideas? Does he understand that the same object can be classified in different ways?

Table 8–4 *(continued)*

	Test Description	Examples of Classroom Observations
Grammatic closure	The child is asked to complete sentences using the correct inflection: e.g., "Here is a dog; here are two [dogs]." "The man is painting. He is a [painter]."	Does the child speak correctly?
Auditory sequential memory	The child is requested to repeat a series of digits presented rapidly.	Can the child, after hearing a spoken sentence or number fact or a word spelled orally, repeat the information?
Visual sequential memory	The child is shown a sequence of geometric forms; it is removed, and the child is asked to reproduce the sequence by placing chips in proper order.	Can the child focus his attention? Can he discriminate among similar geometric forms? Can he copy a pattern? Can he reproduce it from memory?
Visual closure	The child is asked to identify all the partially obscured pictures of common objects against a distracting background; he must do so in 30 seconds.	Does he scan pictures? Can he work rapidly? Is he easily distracted? Can he locate specific information on a printed page? Does he have special difficulty in reading hyphenated words or blurry ditto copies?
Auditory closure (optional)	The child is asked to repeat words or phrases in which certain sounds have been omitted: e.g., "Ea ter unny" (Easter bunny).	Does the child understand a speaker with a different accent? Does he understand phone conversations? Can he understand speech in a noisy room? Does he leave off word endings?
Sound blending (optional)	Sounds are spoken at half-second intervals, and the child must blend them into a word: e.g., "f-oo-t, f-u-n, wh-e-n."	Can the child decode unfamiliar words in reading if he can associate the sound with the individual letter? Can he blend sounds into words, as in the test?

Reprinted from Frostig and Maslow: Learning problems in the classroom. Copyright 1973 by Grune & Stratton.

has to evaluate the meaning of the image or concept formed by the relationship of the words.

The visual reception subtest draws upon the ability to comprehend pictures and to relate the objects denoted by the pictures in a functional manner. For instance, in the subtest the child may observe the picture of a flyswatter for 3 seconds and then look at a page illustrating a fly, a slotted spatula, a tennis racquet, and a can of insect spray. The correct response is to point to the insect spray, which is functionally more like a flyswatter than to the spatula or racquet, both of which are perceptually more similar to the swatter.

The level of auditory receptive abilities may be inferred from observing how well the child can carry out a short verbal direction (when motivated to do so), whether he can recognize common environmental sounds, whether he can learn from listening to a taped story—in short, how well he seems to understand what is heard.

The level of visual receptive abilities may be inferred in analogous fashion. Can specifically required information be obtained from pictures, films, maps, graphs? Does a child know how tools are used? Does the child relate the things that he sees to his own or others' shared experiences?

The ITPA explores only auditory and visual receptive abilities. The classroom teacher may want to know in addition how well the child learns haptically (that is, how well he learns from receiving feedback from his tactile and kinesthetic, or muscle, senses simultaneously, as, for instance, in finger tracing). Some idea of the ability in this respect may be gained by having the child identify by touch common objects contained in an opaque box or bag or by tracing an object. Haptic receptive abilities are necessary for learning by tracing methods.

Verbal and Manual Expression

The ITPA subtests for verbal expression and manual expression assess certain of the child's abilities to express ideas. In the manual expression test the child is shown an object or a picture of an object, and is supposed to show by gesture how it is used. However, this subtest involves not only the ability to express an idea through movement but also motor planning, imagery, and memory. The responses to this subtest will be greatly influenced by the fund of personal experiences. For instance, a ghetto child with excellent ability to express himself through gesture may be totally unable to show how to play the flute because he may never have seen one.

The periods devoted to creative movement in movement education or physical education give the teacher opportunities to see how well a child can express an idea motorically. Class dramas and playing charades provide such opportunities as do such exercises as acting out a story in reading, moving so as to express a musical or poetic mood, and so on.

The ITPA verbal expression subtest is self-descriptive—can the child express ideas through language? The child is asked to describe familiar objects. This subtest alone among those in the basic test battery encourages verbal fluency and divergent thinking: How much can be said about an object? How many ways can it be used?

By noting a child's vocabulary, store of concepts, fluency, and his verbal creativity, a teacher can appraise verbal expression. There are innumerable opportunities during a class day not only to observe verbal ability but also to teach children to express themselves. This can be done by games as well as formal lessons. For example, a "show and tell" period or a game that involves a small group of children sharing all of the ideas associated with an object or situation fosters communication skills and gives the teacher a chance to conduct an informal lesson in language.

Auditory and Visual Association

The two ITPA subtests labeled association—auditory association and visual association—are conceptual tests. The auditory association test is a test of analogies—for example, "Cotton is soft; stones are [hard]." A child who has difficulty in this subtest may have difficulty in classifying and/or explaining his basis of classification.

For the visual association test pictures have to be associated on the basis of functional categories (such as nail and hammer) and conceptual categories (such as apple and milk, both foods). Generally a child who scores low on this subtest will have fewer concepts than his classmates and greater difficulty in shifting sets, that is, in classifying the same object in different ways. The child may, for instance, not be able to understand that a chair is a piece of furniture, and at the same time a wooden object, a four-legged object, a manufactured object, and so forth. He may have difficulty in connecting ideas; for example, though he may know that water freezes at 32°F and that the average winter temperature of a city is 10°, he may still not understand that the river barges don't run in January.

The ITPA does not assess auditory–motor association (responding with a movement to an auditory cue), visual–vocal association (naming something that one sees), and haptic–vocal association (feeling something and naming it). More importantly, visual–vocal association, needed in reading aloud, and visual–auditory association, needed in reading silently, are omitted from the ITPA.

EVALUATING HIGHER COGNITIVE PROCESSES

The Wechsler Intelligence Scale for Children (WISC) [13] was constructed, like the Stanford-Binet Scale, to assess general intelligence, to predict academic performance, and to classify according to IQ level. Whereas the Stanford-Binet [36] provides only a single quantitative score (IQ), the WISC provides scores for six verbal subtests, six performance or nonverbal subtests, and three IQ scores (verbal, performance, and full-scale).

Each subtest of the WISC requires a number of underlying abilities. Moreover, the same basic ability may be required in several subtests. For example, the well-established ability factor "verbal comprehension" is a major ability required in four of the six verbal subtests (information, comprehension, similarities, and vocabulary); attention and concentration are major abilities required in digit span, arithmetic, and coding; and the ability to overcome an embedding context is required in picture completion, block design, and object assembly [37].

WISC Verbal Subtests

The six verbal subtests of the WISC are listed in Table 8-5 with the major abilities that they assess and sample items.

The types of tasks assessed by the WISC can serve as useful guides to the classroom teacher, but one may wish to go beyond them. For example, when a child scores low in the arithmetic subtest (oral arithmetic), the teacher is not interested primarily in the fact that the child cannot solve the problem (in the product of his effort), but in *why* the child cannot solve the problem. Was there failure because the child could not remember the number fact, or because he could not remember the elements, or because he could not visualize the meaning of the verbal statements, or because he could not associate the situational meaning with the required arithmetical operation, or for other reasons? Varying the task requirement may suggest the answer. For example, if the child cannot do the problem when he reads it but can do the same problem presented in pictorial fashion, he may have specific difficulties in visualization.

WISC Performance Subtests

The six performance area subtests of the WISC involve tasks less familiar to the classroom teacher. They are listed in Table 8-6.

Picture completion requires the child to name or point to a missing or incorrectly drawn portion of a figure. Can the child remember what an object looks like even when it is incomplete or partially obscured? Can he make a

Table 8–5

The Verbal Subtests of the Wechsler Intelligence Scale for Children

	Major Ability Assessed	Sample Item
1. Information	General background of knowledge acquired from experiences in the cultural environment.	"How many legs does a cat have?"
2. Similarities	Ability to determine essential relationships (usually of an abstract nature) between two objects or concepts.	"In what way are a cat and a dog alike?"
3. Arithmetic	Ability to concentrate and exert a mental effort utilizing abstract numerical concepts and arithmetic operations.	"How many apples can you buy for 36 cents if one apple costs 4 cents?"
4. Vocabulary	Verbal comprehension, verbal fluency, and word knowledge acquired from environmental experiences.	"What is a horse?"
5. Comprehension	Common sense and judgment regarding the socially accepted action in a given situation.	"What should you do if you see smoke coming from the window of a building?"
6. Digit span	Immediate auditory sequential memory (requires attention and concentration).	"If I say 5–2–4, what would you say?"

mental image of it? Imagery is also tapped in the ITPA subtests of visual closure, manual expression, and verbal expression and in the WISC subtests of arithmetic, object assembly, and block design, and possibly in others. Imagery is essential for understanding the meaning of what is read and for understanding reports on all that is not immediately present to the senses, especially when the comprehension of relationships and of physical and temporal change are involved. The picture completion subtest also requires the child to scan and to detect logical inconsistencies in pictures. Evaluation of pictorial representation is an important learning skill needed in such academic content areas as social studies and science.

Table 8–6

The Performance Subtests of the Wechsler Intelligence Scale for Children

1. Picture completion	Ability to distinguish essential from nonessential details from a visually perceived object from everyday life.	A profile view of a person with an ear missing
2. Picture arrangement	Ability to arrange cartoon like pictorial sequences to make a meaningful story (requires planning and anticipating sequential and causal events).	Three pictures depicting a fight between two men
3. Block design	The ability to analyze an abstract pattern into its parts and to reproduce the parts into an anticipatory image of the whole (requires visual-motor coordination and nonverbal abstract reasoning).	"Reproduce a design of a red V shape on a white background using four red and white blocks."
4. Object assembly	The ability to assemble parts of a known or imagined object into a meaningful whole (requires visual organization, flexibility, and the ability to integrate new clues).	A cut-up puzzle of an apple to be assembled
5. Coding	The ability to learn a new task requiring visual-motor coordination, visual memory, concentration, and speed.	"Write the appropriate symbol in the empty square below each number."
6. Mazes	The ability to plan ahead to reach a goal in a paper-and-pencil maze (requires visual-motor coordination, planning, and delay of impulsive action).	"Draw the corral path from the starting point to the goal."

The teacher can observe the same skills that are evoked by the picture completion subtest by asking the child to find specific information from a picture, to tell the logical story enacted in a silent film, to discriminate among pictures that vary only in detail, to find inconsistencies in verbal descriptions of pictures, and so on.

The arrangement of a series of pictures in correct logical or temporal order is the task of the picture arrangement subtest. Understanding logical and temporal order is basic to understanding both history and science and to evaluating the consequences of one's own or others' behavior in all situations.

The teacher can observe this understanding in the child's responses to academic questions during social studies or science instruction. It is also possible to detect whether children can perceive correct temporal sequences in everyday life (for example, by asking, "What has to be done first, putting the glue on the paper or folding it?"). The understanding of sequences in academic subjects may be strongly influenced by the child's attitude toward school and academic learning and by the child's linguistic functions. Performance in arts and crafts and other manipulative activities does not require verbalization and is not as readily influenced by attitudes toward school learning. Sequential abilities, therefore, should be observed in nonverbal as well as verbal tasks. For instance, the classroom teacher may ask the child to arrange in order a series of comic strip frames, or a series of stick figures that tell an amusing story, or a series of pictures that describe a science or cooking lesson that the child has experienced. Arranging such a series, telling why the pictures have been ordered in such a certain way, or proposing other possible logical ways of arranging them is a means of evaluating the child's verbal and nonverbal abilities and at the same time constitutes an excellent small-group language lesson.

In the block design subtest the child must assemble blocks composed of square and triangular patterns in such a way as to reproduce a design. The ability to analyze and synthesize visual patterns required in this test is the same as that required in such tasks as spelling, reading maps and graphs, and model making.

Observing how a child puts together a model of something in which he is interested (a car, ship, doll house, chemical molecule, or whatever) is one way in which the teacher can check the ability to analyze and synthesize patterns. Many children, however, differ in their ability to perceive two-dimensional objects as opposed to three-dimensional objects. The children, therefore, should also reproduce patterns with pegs, beads, or marbles. Or they may copy such patterns as a Masai beaded necklace, a Byzantine tile, or a Polynesian story board during social studies.

In object assembly the child assembles cardboard pieces in order to complete the picture of a common object. In addition to familiarity with the object and the ability to remember it, this subtest requires analysis of part-whole relationships, mental manipulation, and critical evaluation. The teacher can observe performance as the child fits together classroom puzzles made by cutting pictures into well-defined parts. These puzzles may be integrated with the teaching of academic subjects by choosing pictures showing, for example, the digestive system, a battery circuit, a political map, or a blueprint.

The mazes subtest, which is similar to the pencil-and-paper mazes found in children's activities books, is an optional WISC subtest and is not always given. It involves visualization, planning, the ability to direct and maintain attention, and motor coordination.

For the symbol-substitution subtest the child must substitute certain symbols for others. It has been found to be of special significance, particularly for children with learning difficulties [38]. Coding requires the child to be able to shift attention, direct eye movements, remember something for short periods, handle symbols, perceive position in space and spatial relationships, write easily, and react speedily—all of which influence the acquisition of academic skills. Certainly reading, writing, spelling, and arithmetic involve working with visual symbols.

To evaluate coding ability, the teacher can observe whether the child has special difficulties with such mathematical symbols as $> < - + =$, with reading a map, with algebraic statements, and so on.

Block design, picture arrangement, object assembly, mazes, and coding are timed tests. Often a child fails these tasks not because of a deficiency in the underlying abilities but because of a tendency to "freeze" under pressure, or unfamiliarity with timed tests, or a habitually slow response pattern.

Children with learning difficulties and children from nonindustrial cultural backgrounds frequently have difficulty with timed tests. The teacher's knowledge of the child, and, if necessary, allowing the child to do identical tasks under both open and defined time limits, can pinpoint whether the primary cause of a poor performance is the task itself or the conditions (for example, the time limit) under which the task is performed, or both.

THE PURPOSE OF EVALUATION

Assessment of a child's basic abilities is the indispensable first step in constructing an educational program that will help the child to develop all his psychological functions and to achieve academically. The developmental sequence described in Chapter 7 can serve as the evaluative framework to ensure that assessment of abilities is relatively complete, balanced and integrated. As described in this chapter, both standardized tests and teacher observations are needed to pinpoint each child's specific strengths and weaknesses.

It cannot be repeated too often nor stressed enough that evaluation procedures should be conducted not for the purpose of categorizing children but to serve as the basis for instituting an optimal educational program.

Educational programing based on the results of a developmental assessment must be, like a good evaluation, balanced and integrated. Such programing is both an art and a science. The case histories in Chapter 9 illustrate certain principles, common problems, and the operation of what can only be called empathy, intuition, and commitment to the overall needs of the child.

REFERENCES

1. Meeker M: The Structure of Intellect. Columbus, Ohio, Merrill, 1969
2. Sheppard M: A Teacher's School Entry Screening Test. Mosman, Austral. Specific Learning Difficulties Association of New South Wales, 1972
3. de Hirsch K, Jansky J, Langford W: Predicting Reading Failure. New York, Harper & Row, 1966
4. Pate J, Webb W: The First-Grade Screening Test. Minneapolis, American Guidance Service, 1966
5. Meier JH, Cozier VO, Giles MT: Individual Learning Disabilities Classroom Screening Instrument. Evergreen, Colo., Learning Pathways, 1970.
6. Board of Education, City of New York: Let's Look at Children. Princeton, N.J., Educational Testing Service, 1965
7. Caldwell BM: Cooperative Preschool Inventory (rev ed). Princeton, N.J., Educational Testing Service, 1970
8. Educational Testing Service: CIRCUS: A Comprehensive Program of Assessment Services for Preprimary Children. Princeton, N.J., the Service, 1974
9. Orpet R: Frostig Movement Skills Test Battery (exp ed). Palo Alto, Calif., Consulting Psychologists Press, 1972
10. Frostig M, Lefever DW, Whittlesey JRB: The Marianne Frostig Developmental Test of Visual Perception. Palo Alto, Calif., Consulting Psychologists Press, 1964
11. Wepman J: Wepman Test of Auditory Discrimination. Chicago, Language Research Associates, 1958
12. Kirk SA, McCarthy JJ, Kirk WD: The Illinois Test of Psycholinguistic Abilities (rev ed). Urbana, University of Illinois Press, 1968
13. Wechsler D: Revised Wechsler Intelligence Scale for Children. New York, The Psychological Corporation, 1974
14. Orpet R, Meyers CE: Consistency of psychomotor factors in the Frostig Movement Skills Battery in seven age groups, paper presented at the meeting of the American Psychological Association, 1972
15. Kraus H: Kraus-Weber Test for Minimum Muscular Fitness. Therapeutic Exercises. Springfield, Ill., Thomas, 1963
16. Roach EG, Kephart NC: The Purdue Perceptual-Motor Survey. Columbus, Ohio, Merrill, 1966

17. Sloan W: The Lincoln-Oseretsky Motor Development Scale. Chicago, Stoelting, 1955

18. Cratty BJ, Martin MM: Perceptual-Motor Efficiency in Children: The Measurement and Improvement of Movement Attributes. Philadelphia, Lea and Febiger, 1969

19. Orpet, R., Heustis TL: Move-Grow-Learn Movement Skills Survey. Chicago, Follett, 1971

20. Frostig M: Move-Grow-Learn. Chicago, Follett, 1969

21. Nicks DC, Fleishman EA: What Do Physical Tests Measure—A Review of Factor Analytic Studies. Technical Report I, prepared for the Office of Naval Research. New Haven, Yale University Press, 1960

22. Guilford JP: A system of psychomotor abilities. Am J Psychol 71:164–174, 1958

23. Frostig M: Movement Education: Theory and Practice. Chicago, Follett, 1970, pp 32–33

24. Bilodeau EA: Acquisition of Skill. New York, Academic Press, 1966

25. Frostig M, Horne D, Miller A: Pictures and Patterns: Teacher's Guides and Workbooks (rev ed). Chicago, Follett, 1972

26. Roswell FG, Chall JS: Roswell-Chall Auditory Blending Test. New York, Essay Press, 1963

27. Spache GD: Diagnostic Reading Scales. New York, McGraw-Hill, 1960

28. Thurstone LL: A Factorial Study of Perception. Psychometric Monographs (4). Chicago, University of Chicago Press, 1944

29. Wedell K: Variations in perceptual ability among types of cerebral palsy. Cerebral Palsy Bulletin 2:149–157, 1960

30. Cruickshank WM, Bice HV, Wallen NE: Perception and Cerebral Palsy. Syracuse, N.Y., Syracuse University Press, 1957

31. Koppitz EM: The Bender Gestalt Test for Young Children. New York, Grune & Stratton, 1964

32. Goodenough F.: Draw-a-Man Test. The Measurement of Intelligence by Drawings. Yonkers-on-Hudson, N.Y., World Book, 1962

33. Bateman BD: Interpretation of the 1961 Illinois Test of Psycholinguistic Abilities. Seattle, Special Child Publications, 1968

34. Osgood CE: A behavioristic analysis of perception and language as cognitive phenomena, in Bruner J (ed.): Contemporary Approaches to Cognition. Cambridge, Harvard University Press, 1957

35. Kirk SA, Kirk WD: Psycholinguistic Learning Disabilities: Diagnosis and Remediation. Urbana, University of Illinois Press, 1971

36. Terman LM, Merrill M: Stanford-Binet Intelligence Test. Manual for the Third Revision: Form L-M. Boston, Houghton Mifflin, 1960

37. Witkin HA, Dyk RB, Faterson HF, Goodenough DR, Karp SA: Psychological Differentiation. New York, John Wiley, 1962

38. Tyson M: A comparison of the abilities of normal and subnormal children to match and discriminate figures. Unpublished doctoral dissertation, University of London, 1961

9
Examples of Individualized Programing

We have several generations of work to do before concluding that any child . . . who does not think well under one set of conditions cannot be taught how to do so when the conditions are changed.

Sylvia Farnham-Diggory [1, p 80]

The terms *program* and *programing* often refer to the step-by-step teaching of skills and content material. In this book, *individualized programing* is used to indicate the planning of individualized instruction, including curriculum, counseling techniques, teaching methods, and classroom management.

Individualized programs are based on the knowledge gained about the child through testing, observations made by the teacher, and parent interviews. We have stressed that testing is a valuable part of the diagnostic procedure only if it is followed by a prescription of teaching methods and remedial procedures and only if the child's physical development, life space, and interactions with the environment, past and present, are also taken into account. This is the basic philosophy upon which the programing is done for each child who is brought to the Marianne Frostig Center for Educational Therapy. The five basic tests * administered at the Frostig Center and observational methods have been discussed at length. Other tests are administered when deemed necessary to supplement the information derived from the basic tests. In addition, initial observation, at least during a "tutoring-observation hour," is regarded as indispensable. It not only constitutes an essential element in the diagnostic

*The Frostig Movement Skills Test Battery, the Marianne Frostig Developmental Test of Visual Perception, the Wepman Test of Auditory Discrimination, the Illinois Test of Psycholinguistic Abilities, and the Wechsler Intelligence Scale for Children.

procedures, but it can also be used therapeutically to correct disabilities and show the child that he really is able to learn so that he will have confidence in his new program.

The teacher who is confronted with the task of developing the optimum potential of a child or of remedying failure is usually confronted with the child's inability to do complex tasks. For example, Sue may not be able to answer a comprehension question about her text. She may not be able to put the events of the story in the right order; she may not be able to make inferences; she may not be able to remember events read in previous chapters. These are most complex tasks, and it is not possible to state with certainty exactly why these tasks are difficult for her. In like fashion, the scores of intelligence tests, especially verbal tests, do not pinpoint the causes of a child's difficulties. Clues to the reasons for a child's failures can be found only by observing the child's behavior in other tasks and by careful analysis of the test profile whenever it is available.

The developmental sequence provides both procedure and guidelines. The teacher has to ask whether a child's difficulties with a complex task may

Fig. 9-1.   The teacher must keep a continuous record of the child's behavior and must utilize information about what the child knows as well as any mistakes he may make in planning lesson sequences. (Photo by James Quinn and Michael Campa.)

stem from a failure in sensorimotor functions, visual or auditory perceptual skills, language skills, or the integration of the various stimuli that impinge on the child or whether it is due to a lack of prerequisite academic skills needed to complete the task or a combination of these factors. The evaluative methods described in the preceding chapter can be used to formulate tentative answers to this question.

Three examples of how evaluation and observation can be used to develop individual programs are given in this chapter. The first, concerning Shali, demonstrates the importance of classroom observation as well as formal test results in developing initial teaching strategies. The second, that of Libby, shows that some children can be helped optimally only if a complete evaluation is made, even if these children seem to have only delimited problems. If Libby had not been given the Frostig Movement Skills Test Battery or if she had been observed only in the reading situation, her basic difficulties would not have been analyzed and she would not have received the most effective help. The third example of individualized programing concerns Daryl, a child with several problems, the relative importance of which the teacher had to weigh in deciding the priorities and emphases of training. Daryl needed help in overcoming his emotional disturbances caused by his failure in school; he needed careful step-by-step procedures to learn school tasks so that he could hold his own with other children; and he needed intensive basic ability training. The teacher met these needs by giving priority first to one area and then to another, but always keeping the goals of his overall program in mind.

These three examples of programing based on test results are followed by examples of responses to emotional and social problems of varying degrees of severity that were closely observed, analyzed, and responded to by the teacher or school official. The first of these indicates how classroom structure can be changed to take the observed needs of a youngster into account; the others are essentially demonstrations of the effectiveness of intelligent participation in a caring relationship in response to various kinds of needs.

SHALI

Shali, who was 8½ years old when first referred to the Center, has intelligence scores that would place her into the low normal range. She is small for her age, narrow-boned, and slender. Her tiny face is flanked by two bushy, blonde ponytails. She has a compliant demeanor and seems to want to appear obedient and polite. As long as no demands are put on her, she gives no indication of her mastery of techniques of refusal and her ability to escape from any task that she dislikes.

School History

Shali's parents state that they noticed no problems until Shali entered kindergarten. Her developmental milestones (when she began to sit up, walk, talk, and so forth) were all in the average range, and her behavior as a preschooler was described as that of a "cute little girl, sometimes a bit mischievous."

In her kindergarten year, however, Shali often came home upset from school, especially when her regular teacher was ill and there was a substitute. On these occasions she said that she did not want to go to school.

In the first grade the teacher felt that Shali was slow in learning. She therefore recommended that Shali repeat the first grade, but her mother refused. During the next year Shali was reported to be well below grade level and unwilling to participate in reading, math, and other academic subjects.

All of the reports of Shali's teachers were similar: Shali resisted schoolwork. When she felt a task to be hard and thought she might not succeed, she indulged in the pretense that she did not care how her work was executed and substituted scribbling, looking at pictures in a book, or any other activity connected with the task except doing the task itself. Her favorite escape was to let her gaze rove around the room instead of looking at her work. "Pretend performances" or frank evasion were evident whenever Shali felt afraid of failure.

Home Environment

Shali's mother had been thought to be unable to have children; therefore, she and her husband adopted two children. These children—a girl, now 17½, and a boy, 16½ years old—seem to be well-adjusted teenagers.

When Shali was born, her parents were overjoyed and lavished much affection on her. However, this happy state only lasted until about the time that Shali entered school, when the mother's physical and mental health, which had been borderline, began to break down. Both parents continued to love Shali and to fondle her, but at times when the mother was ill, Shali was totally ignored. Shali would then withdraw and become fidgety and restless, to which the parents would respond by admonishing her. This state of affairs accounted for her dependence upon the presence of her regular teacher in kindergarten. It was unfortunate that this teacher, like her own mother, was often ill and absent. Whenever this was the case, Shali cried, pouted, and resisted all discipline. She felt isolated at home and insecure at school and often abandoned at both places.

During the time that she was in first grade Shali developed temper tantrums, which were controlled at home by putting her to bed and in school by not requiring any work. When Shali was in second grade, her mother's health became worse; so did Shali's depression and fits of anger. Whenever the mother felt pressured, she fainted, and she finally made a suicide attempt. During the height of the mother's illness the parents became very hostile to each other.

About a year before Shali was brought to the Frostig Center for Educational Therapy the parents began psychological treatment. According to their therapist's report, they are now better able to discuss differences of opinion and to treat Shali more consistently. Nevertheless, the mother is still rather anxious and tense. There are still differences of opinion between her and her husband, and Shali remains an essentially lonely little girl.

Evaluation

Because of her inability to function in school, Shali has been tested numerous times from kindergarten on. Each time the psychologist has reported that her IQ test score was about 90 but that her IQ might well be higher if she were willing to try. All examiners have agreed that the emotional factors in Shali's school failure are significant but that they are not the only causes. Two main sets of factors seem to play a role in Shali's school difficulties. One, as noted, is her emotional disturbance and the other is the definite lags in certain abilities as indicated by her test results (see Figure 9–2). Usually the emotional factors enhance minor learning difficulties until they become unsurmountable obstacles.

Shali's very poor performance in tasks requiring fine motor coordination, especially in bimanual coordination (bead stringing) and in crossing the midline of her body (block transfer), and the divergent scores of one-foot balance with open and closed eyes, as well as her deficits in verbal areas and in auditory and visual perception and the reports received from various clinicians, indicate a probable neurological dysfunction. However, these deficits in psychological functions might not have impaired the child's school performance so severely had they not been accompanied by her emotional reactions to the school environment as well as to her own deficits. Her motivation had been particularly affected, and she tried to escape learning.

There were also factors in the home environment that reinforced her escape mechanisms. Fear of learning is to be expected in children who know that they are failing, but the inability to overcome this fear and the use of well-defined escape mechanisms occur most often when parental anxiety is transferred to and assimilated by the child. This seemed to be the situation with Shali.

Initial Evaluation and Educational Planning

The initial evaluation suggests approaches regarding the overall treatment program of a child. For Shali, treatment of the parents (especially the mother's

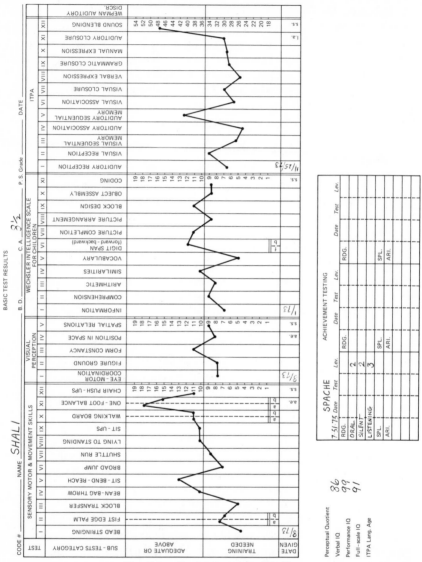

Fig. 9-2.   Basic test results: Shali.

emotional disturbance), treatment of the emotional and behavioral component in Shali's refusal to learn, treatment of the real underlying deficits, and amelioration of the academic deficits through the use of specific teaching methods were all of importance.

The public school authorities had decided that transfer to a special school was necessary because Shali's achievement was far below the required minimum, and her behavior was unsatisfactory. Therefore, she was transferred to the Marianne Frostig Center of Educational Therapy. The parents remained in treatment with the therapist whom they had engaged.

Since Shali's emotional disturbance was strongly tied in with her learning difficulties, it was decided to undertake her whole treatment within the classroom, at least for a few months. Her initial test results would guide the different aspects of her educational treatment; this treatment, of course, would be continuously evaluated in the classroom and changed whenever indicated.

Sensorimotor Functions

The evaluation of sensorimotor functions with the Frostig Movement Skills Test Battery [2] had shown that Shali was far below the expected proficiency in tasks requiring fine motor coordination—bead stringing and transferring blocks from the left to the right side of her body. Her low scores could not be ascribed to resistance because she had been unaware of her difficulties and had enjoyed these tasks, which she thought to be easy.

Low scores in both bead stringing and block transfer are found very frequently in children with learning difficulties; in fact, they are often the lowest scores of the battery. Difficulty with bead stringing indicates poor eye-hand coordination in bimanual tasks, and performance with this task is often poorer than with the sequential movements required in the tasks done with one hand (fist-edge-palm). Bimanual coordination requires smooth coordinated functioning of the right and left hemispheres of the brain, which is also necessary in the block-transfer task. The specific difficulties in crossing the midline and in bimanual tasks that children with learning difficulties frequently display have been observed by Newell Kephart [3] and others working with these children. The significance of this deficit is being studied by many researchers interested in brain physiology and psychoneurology. At the Frostig Center we try to ameliorate the disturbance by emphasizing exercises that require crossing the midline [4] and bimanual exercises.

Shali's difficulty in crossing the midline was also observed in the classroom. For example, when Shali wanted to pick up with her left hand a crayon that lay to her right on the desk, she would turn her body so as to avoid reaching across the midline.

Shali's hand dominance was not yet established. She usually preferred the left hand. She had poor perception of position in space, which is very common in children who have no established dominance, and she could not differentiate between such letters as *b* and *d* or *p* and *q*. Therefore, an effort was made to establish dominance.

Observation also showed that Shali's difficulty in fine motor coordination seemed to stem from a lack of right-left coordination rather than from a lack of finger dexterity. Thus she needed practice in manipulating small objects with both hands. It was suggested that in arithmetic she work with blocks that could be clipped together and taken apart only by using both hands.* (The rods used by some other children could be manipulated with one hand.)

Shali's ability to skip and jump was observed further. She needed practice with movements requiring leg strength, but she had no difficulty with asymmetrical movements, such as those involved in galloping.

Shali's other scores on the Frostig Movement Skills Test Battery were generally in the average range. She performed well in tasks that require balance and flexibility.

Visual Perception

The Frostig Developmental Test of Visual Perception and the Bender Visual Motor Gestalt Test were used to evaluate visual perception. Shali's scores on these tests were poor. On the Bender Gestalt Test she showed numerous distortions, rotations, and general spatial confusion. Her score on the eye-motor subtest of the Frostig Developmental Test of Visual Perception was low, confirming the evidence from the Frostig Movement Skills Test Battery: Shali had poor fine motor coordination.

Figure-ground perception, perception of position in space, and perception of spatial relationships were also impaired. It was, therefore, decided to introduce visual perceptual training, using the worksheets and teacher's guide of the Frostig Developmental Program for Visual Perception.

Auditory Perception

Auditory perception may be evaluated by the Wepman Test of Auditory Discrimination and by subtests of the WISC and the ITPA. The information, comprehension, similarities, and even the arithmetic subtests of the WISC give clues to the child's understanding of spoken language. The WISC digit span subtest evaluates immediate auditory memory (digit span forward) and also mental manipulation of auditorily perceived sequences (digit span backward). The ITPA evaluates various aspects of auditory perception more directly and in more detail in its subtests of auditory reception, auditory memory, auditory association, and auditory closure. Thus the subtests of the WISC and the ITPA together with the Wepman (which taps the ability to discriminate among speech sounds in words) give much insight into the child's auditory perceptual func-

*Unifix Interlocking Cubes, available from A. Daigger & Company, 657 Oak Grove Plaza, Menlo Park, Calif. 94025, are examples.

tions. Careful evaluation of the child's verbal expression during testing and in the classroom gives additional information.

However, certain more specific although informal tests of the child's perception of spoken language should always be added. It is very important, for instance, to ascertain whether the child can perceive word boundaries; that is, to perceive where a word begins and ends. To evaluate this, the child can be asked to indicate the number of words in a spoken sentence. Very simple sentences consisting only of nouns and verbs should be used as a first step. For example, the child might be asked to repeat the separate words in a sentence, such as "children play." The second-step task might be indicate the separate words in a three-word sentence, such as "children play together" or "all children play." For the third step, the child would be asked to indicate the individual words in a sentence containing words necessary for correct grammatical structuring but which have no meaning by themselves, such as "I play with you" or "Susie and I play" or "the tree has pretty leaves." Shali had difficulties in identifying words at the second and third steps.

Another such informal test can evaluate the child's ability to remember sequences of words. A game can be played between an adult and a child or among a group of children in which at each step or turn the preceding sequence must be reproduced exactly and another word in the relevant category added. For example:

Player 1:   I am going on a trip. I will take a coat.
Player 2:   I am going on a trip. I will take a coat and an umbrella.
Player 1:   I am going on a trip. I will take a coat, an umbrella, and a suitcase.
Player 2:   I am going on a trip. I will take a coat, an umbrella, a suitcase, and a hat.

Shali's memory for such a sequence was rather poor. In the sequence game played with a number of children, she was one of the first to make a mistake.

Evaluation of Higher Cognitive Functions and Language: The WISC and ITPA

Higher cognitive functions were evaluated with the Wechsler Intelligence Scale for Children (WISC).* With the exception of similarities, digit span (memory for auditory stimuli), block design (analysis and synthesis of patterns), and picture completion (memory for details) Shali's scores were slightly or markedly below average, with the lowest scores in information and vocabulary. The discrepancy between verbal and performance scores was 13 points. This indicated that Shali's major difficulties were in the verbal area, although she also had significant sensorimotor and visual perceptual difficulties.

*The 1949 edition of the WISC was used.

Both information and vocabulary subtest scores are strongly influenced by school learning. It may well be that Shali's aversion to the school situation had depressed her scores, but the low scores on the Illinois Test of Psycholinguistic Abilities (ITPA) indicated that this was not the only reason for her failure. Vocabulary and information subtests are highly correlated,* and are best developed together. Exercises that children experience as boring should always be avoided, especially with a resisting child like Shali. To develop Shali's vocabulary and information, it was suggested that there be systematic teaching in science and social studies, using multimodal presentation (listening to explanations while looking at filmstrips, slides, pictures, maps, and so on; making graphs, drawings, and pictographs; and writing down or discussing what she learned).

Shali's lowest WISC score was in arithmetic. Mathematics are difficult for children with poor visual perceptual skills. It was hoped that visual perceptual training would help to improve her scores. The auditory sequential memory subtest of the ITPA and the digit span subtest of the WISC were high, indicating that she could learn auditorily and that she could remember what she learned; observation confirmed this. These abilities could be utilized in teaching her arithmetic, particularly number facts.

Psycholinguistic functions were evaluated with the ITPA [5, 6], which includes subtests that tap perceptual and higher cognitive abilities as well as language functions in the usual meaning of the term. There is, therefore, an overlap with other tests in the battery. Economically, the administration of the total battery may seem a decided disadvantage; but it is an advantage insofar as comparison of subtests evaluating similar functions makes it possible to obtain differences in the scores that pinpoint the difficulty. For instance, lower scores on the WISC digit span forward subtest than on the ITPA auditory sequential memory subtest may indicate that a child has a difficulty in "chunking" (grouping).

Shali's ITPA subtest scores showed many deficits, especially in visual sequential memory, in associational skills (auditory association, visual association), and in expressive abilities (verbal expression, grammatic closure, and manual expression). These scores gave additional indications regarding this child's training needs.

Since visual sequential memory was low while auditory sequential memory was high (as indicated by the ITPA subtest and the digit span subtest of the WISC), memory tasks during academic learning should be presented to Shali auditorily. Number triads ("number facts") and measurement tables and spelling are examples. Visual and kinesthetic learning should not be neglected, but they should always be enhanced by auditory presentation. Training in

*A correlation of 0.65 was found between these two subtests for a sample of 111 children between the ages of 6–9 and 8–9 enrolled at the Frostig Center for full-time schooling.

memory for visual sequences should be done separately also—first with pictures and geometric forms, later with letters, words, and numbers.

The visual and auditory association subtests require concept formation and the drawing of conclusions. Both were difficult for Shali. The categorization program developed by Aurelia Levi [7, 8] and the attribute games [9] were suggested to develop classification, categorization, concept formation, and logical thinking.

Shali's deficits in verbal expression and grammatic closure (grammatically correct speech) can be ameliorated through much practice in speech and writing. Deficits in auditory closure make spelling difficult because not all letters are heard in their correct order. Specific exercises in phonetic spelling (often with the use of nonsense words) that introduce consonants, vowels, and blends systematically can lead to improvement. These were planned for Shali. It was suggested to her teacher that she should always speak slowly, distinctly, and simply when giving instructions to Shali.

The ITPA also indicated two specific strengths. Shali had received intensive phonic training in public school, and this was reflected in her ITPA subtest score in sound blending; it was one of her highest scores, despite the generally low scores in subtests involving auditory perceptual skills. Her other strength was in auditory memory, which has already been discussed.

Whenever a test battery is administered, not only should every test score be evaluated by itself, but also there should be an evaluation of the relationships among the subtest scores of the different tests in the battery, for they provide valuable indications of the child's strengths and weaknesses. We have pointed out, for instance, that the digit span subtest of the WISC (and the separate forward and backward scores) and the memory for auditory sequences of the ITPA should always be compared.

Evaluation during the Initial Tutoring Hour

Observations of the child's learning style are equally important as test results. For instance, the results of the sensorimotor and movement skills battery, the eye-motor coordination subtest of the visual perception test, and the manual expression subtest of the ITPA indicated that Shali needed manipulatory activities. During school work these deficits were exaggerated because Shali's unwillingness to be involved in academic tasks made her appear even slower and more clumsy than her behavior during testing had indicated. The teacher had to find the optimum way to include manipulatory tasks in the curriculum, and also had to select optimal strategies to motivate Shali to "get moving."

The deficits in information, comprehension, vocabulary, verbal expression, and grammatic closure indicated that language activity should accompany

all training in visual perceptual and sensorimotor areas and that ample opportunity for language activities, including oral language, should be provided.
Subsequently the teacher had to observe how Shali could be induced to
accompany her work with visual perceptual training materials with a great deal
of language expression. A listless child often refuses to engage in verbal as well
as motor expression. Whenever possible play had to be used to make Shali
willing to talk and to act.

Such integrative ability training was begun during the observation-
tutoring hour. Shali was given a worksheet from *Pictures and Patterns* [10].
This particular sheet (Figure 9–2) was chosen because it focuses on
figure-ground perception, in which Shali scored low, and because the picture
was related to a poem that Shali was asked to read that she thought funny.

First, Shali was asked to name the animals that she saw, then to count
them, and then to say what sounds they made. Next a transparent plastic
(acetate) sheet was placed over the picture, and Shali was asked to trace the
outline of each animal in turn. Using a sheet on which erasures could easily be
made protected her from failure and also gave the opportunity for extra practice
in eye-motor coordination. She at first omitted the duck's foot, but when asked
to which animal the foot could belong, she revealed her ability to visualize and
completed the tracing correctly. However, she was unable to say why the
webbed foot was helpful to a duck. The importance of the webbing for moving
in the water was explained. (Training in eye-hand coordination and
figure-ground perception, language, and conceptual thinking was thus integrated into one task.) When Shali had traced each animal correctly, the acetate
sheet was removed, and she traced directly on the paper.

The teacher and Shali then discussed briefly how each of the animals
moved in its natural environment. Shali was asked to move like a duck on land
and then like a duck in water; these exercises in motor expression she enjoyed
greatly and she became quite animated. Next she was asked if she had any of the
animals as a pet, to which she answered that she had a cat. She was encouraged
to talk about her cat. Training in motor expression (more specifically in
coordination, flexibility and motor planning), visualization, and verbal expression were integrated in this task.

Throughout this session auditory, visual, and perceptual-motor tasks
(using kinesthetic input) were provided. Classification was not included in this
training because it was more important during the beginning sessions to induce
Shali to express herself. At a later stage the teacher might have asked which
animals were tame and which wild, which were mammals, which were birds,
and so forth. Classification exercises and games developing concepts were
important for Shali, but at this point observation showed a greater need for
verbal expression.

The test scores not only give some clues regarding the basic training in abilities required by a child, they also indicate how the training in academic skills should be conducted. For Shali, integration of all language skills —speaking, reading, and writing—was deemed to be most important. Shali's lowest scores on the WISC were in information and vocabulary; her ITPA scores also indicated very poor use of language. Consequently, reading material was provided that supplied terms and concepts adequate for Shali's ability. She was asked to use newly acquired words in sentences and stories, to put them in a "word bank," and to use them in games.

During one of the first sessions a short poem was read together by Shali and her teacher. The poem gave her the vocabulary to denote the noises animals make, an exercise she had done previously when working with the visual perception work sheet. She learned that a chicken clucks, a dog barks, a lion roars, and so on. After she had mastered this, a game was played in which the words for the animals and for their vocal production had to be paired. The teacher then wrote the name of the animal, and Shali wrote a word indicating the "noise"; then the roles were reversed. This was done because of Shali's apparent difficulties in forming associations, which were evidenced by her responses to the WISC vocabulary subtest and the association subtest of the ITPA.

Shali's relatively high scores in picture completion and block design and her only slightly depressed scores in coding and object assembly indicate that she had the ability to visualize and to form visual associations. These abilities were utilized in the exercise described. Shali would be helped to acquire vocabulary, information, and reading and writing skills, using visualization and auding as mediators.

The low score in visual sequential memory was not convincing and not in accord with the picture obtained from other test results and from observations. This fact illustrates again how important it is to evaluate the subtest scores in relation to each other and in relation to classroom observations. It might have been that during this subtest Shali indulged in the practice of what she herself termed "eyes going everywhere."

Although auditory memory was Shali's greatest asset, a method of learning to spell and to read was employed that made use of both auditory and visual memory simultaneously. Each new word is color coded, each successive sound being written in a different color, for instance r ea ch—black r, red ea, brown ch). Digraphs, dipthongs, and silent letters are pointed out. Silent letters are written in a stippled fashion. The word "more," for example, might be written with a black m, blue o, red r and stippled e (more). After writing the words in color, they are written with black ink so that synthesis follows the analytic process. The whole word is read after it has been divided into sounds. Shali learned to look at the words, to memorize the nonphonetic elements by remembering their graphic representation, and to reproduce them from memory. She was able to learn to read and spell a sizable number of words during the first two tutoring hours, but only when no more than four distinct speech sounds were involved. To strengthen her visual sequential memory, self-correcting materials and games were used.

Another emphasis in regard to language functions was on recording (taking notes).* Recording is always necessary so that the child can review what has been learned and so that written language can mediate the child's thoughts and assist in the development of cognitive abilities.

Shali received low scores in the auditory association and visual association subtests of the ITPA, which tap higher cognitive functions, especially the abilities of classification, class inclusion, and shifting sets, all necessary for solving the problems posed in these subtests. Yet Shali achieved an adequate score in the similarities subtest of the WISC, which is supposed to evaluate the same abilities. This apparent contradiction occurs quite often. The explanation may be that the first items in similarities did not require problem solving; the responses could be given automatically. (The revised WISC has substituted more difficult items in this subtest.) Some of the easier tasks were based partly on perceptual functions and partly on associative learning. The latter occurs during the classification games and exercises that are part of the regular school curriculum in kindergarten and in the beginning elementary grades.

For Shali, as for other children who show similar difficulties at early age levels, the remedy appears to lie in emphasizing language development, but without neglecting visual perceptual training. If such training is neglected, the child's language development will be retarded. The ability to perceive multiple relationships (evaluated by the association subtests), and other thought processes, will develop better after both basic perceptual and language abilities are acquired.

Children who have failed in school have to be taught skills needed for classroom learning that are usually taken for granted. For example, the ability to listen and to pay attention, the ability to understand the meaning of commonly used words, and the ability to remember what has been shown repeatedly are necessary for success in school. In concentrating on reinforcing their abilities the teacher too often overlooks more specific disabilities that make adaptation to the school environment difficult. For instance, children with disabilities in eye-motor coordination, fine motor coordination, visual perception, and motor planning, frequently have difficulty in copying from the vertical plane of the chalkboard to the horizontal plane of the paper on the desk. This was the case with Shali.

To ameliorate this difficulty, the transposition into another plane had to be taught step by step, beginning with three-dimensional objects. Shali was asked

---

*Recording also includes graphing, map making, and scorekeeping.

to copy random patterns of beads displayed on an abacus propped vertically in front of her onto another abacus lying flat on the table. After this task had become easy, Shali was asked to copy the bead patterns with a pencil. She then learned step by step to copy various patterns, letters, words, sentences, and mathematical examples from a small chalkboard propped on her desk in front of her. Later on, she copied from the regular chalkboard.

Teaching Reading

Some reading methods that were used for Shali have been described in relation to methods employed in teaching information, concepts, and vocabulary. The reading material given her was selected from various fields of interest and subject matter. Some very easy materials were included so that Shali could experience pleasure from reading and would be motivated to put effort into more difficult reading tasks. The easy reading also promoted fluency.

At the beginning of instruction high first-grade material was chosen for Shali. She made only one mistake while reading two stories, but her reading was so labored that it was decided not to use more difficult material until she had

Fig. 9-3. Worksheet used with Shali that focuses on figure–ground perception.

achieved some fluency and a better ability to pay attention—about three or four weeks. Shali read one story a day by reading in alternation with another child who was a good reader; that is, Shali read a short paragraph, then the other child read the next one, and so on. This method was indicated because Shali seemed to tire very easily when reading alone, while her attention wandered when reading with a group.

Teaching Arithmetic

No math test scores were available for Shali. The report from public school stated that Shali was working on a beginner's level and therefore accurate scores could not be obtained.

Children who have difficulties in the first three subtests of the Frostig Movement Skills Test Battery and in visual perception frequently have difficulties in learning mathematical concepts. Observation showed that Shali could not add or subtract because she did not understand partial counting. She drew a new number line for each new addition problem and counted all the dots. Thus, her representation of the problem would be

$$7 + 4 = \vdots \quad \vdots$$

$$5 + 7 = \vdots \quad \vdots$$

This cumbersome procedure had made it impossible for her to keep up with the other children. Partial counting forward and backward was taught successfully during the first two lessons, using step-by-step procedures. Shali first solved problems involving adding and subtracting one, and learned that the correct solution of these problems was the same as counting forward and backward. Then she learned to "skip" one or two numbers and thus to add or subtract two or three. She was then required to write the problems; finally they were practiced again in a card game.

Writing

Shali could not form all letters but could copy them. Since she had difficulties with differentiating between *b* and *d*, the teacher made the following drawing: **b-e-d.** "These letters make a picture of a bed," she said. "Do you see how there is a board at each end, and the rest of the picture makes a mattress? You could not write the *b* or the *d* any other way or the mattress would fall down. So when you hear *b* or *d* in a word, always ask yourself if the letter sounds like the first or last letter in the word *bed*. Then you will be able to write it correctly."

Shali had fair visualization skills and could hear single beginning or final consonants in short words. Consequently, she was able to write without mistake the phonic words beginning or ending with *b* or *d* that the teacher dictated—"bed–mad–Dan–ball–dab–bud–did–dot." No reversals were noted during the remainder of the hour.

Summary of Observations Concerning Shali

Shali's deficits were multiple. In addition to her disabilities, there were attitudinal factors that made progress in public school impossible. In a clinical school, however, the prognosis for Shali was good, provided she could be induced to apply her energy to the learning task instead of evading it. She had to accept help before she could gain the skills in which she was lagging. This was possible in a small class, especially one with a "family" structure, where she could obtain attentive help from the teacher and also from some older, more advanced children.

For Shali, any kind of behavior modification would not have been successful because she got so much pleasure from her passive resistance. She strongly defended against any feelings of trust and love because of her periodical deprivation. Therefore, the only way to get her to work was to make learning intrinsically pleasurable by continuously giving her the feeling of mastery and by concentrating on her interests. At the same time her progress was contingent on her rapport with the teacher who encouraged closeness and tried to foster a warm relationship. In this the teacher was never completely successful, and Shali remained somewhat aloof.

The curriculum for Shali had to follow that of the public school as much as possible. Methods of teaching had to be directed toward helping Shali acquire the abilities she needed for further progress, while at the same time her assets had to be used for learning academic skills.

The importance of movement education for a child like Shali is easily underestimated. The exercises mentioned in this chapter are very critical. The author agrees fully with Kephart's point of view that the amelioration of motor deficits should be emphasized in training [3].

Shali's expressive and creative abilities also had to be considered. Movement education, art, and language activities, including pantomime and drama, were incorporated into the program to help her develop her communicative skills.

As has been indicated, techniques of classroom management were of greatest importance. Shali needed a great deal of teacher contact and approval.

She had to be guided rather than pressured, but she had to be required to finish whatever tasks she began. At first she was given tasks that she regarded as easy, but she had to learn from the beginning that only "results," a finished piece of work, were acceptable. She had to learn to put forth consistently a real, not a pretend effort. After the first tutoring-observation session she said spontaneously, "I learned a lot. I kept my eyes on my work. I like that."

It had been mentioned that counseling for the parents was not instituted at the school because the parents had therapy elsewhere. The teacher did keep in contact with them to help them understand Shali's difficulties and to provide reassurance regarding her progress.

Follow-up

A year after Shali's first observation-tutoring session her IQ remained stable as measured by the WISC; her academic achievement test scores were approximately at age-grade level. After the regular school year at the Frostig Center Shali attended summer school and academically was then ready to return to public school. It was decided, however, that it would be best for her to remain at the clinical school for another year to permit her to consolidate her gains before being required to cope with the stress of transfer to a new situation. As an intermediate step, she may attend summer school at the public school so that she can become accustomed to new surroundings, people, and approaches with relatively little pressure. Her ultimate development will depend to a considerable degree on the stability of her home environment, especially on her mother's physical and emotional health.

Shali's programing has been discussed in much detail because of the complexity of her interacting difficulties. The following individual programs are reported more briefly because the problems are relatively less complicated.

LIBBY

Libby provides an example of a child with very specific learning difficulties. She was 7 years old when referred for tutoring. Libby is a pretty girl, with a small face framed by dark hair. She is thin and shy, and has a very serious demeanor, and is most compliant. Her health has always been good. Her home environment seems pleasant; the parents are concerned and loving.

She was referred by her public school teacher because she reversed letters and words in writing, was a poor speller, and her handwriting was illegible.

Libby was a breach birth and forceps were used. Early development was somewhat slow. She crawled at 10 months, walked at 15 months, and said her first words (other than "dada" and "mama") at 2 years and her first sentence at

2½ years. Libby adjusted well in kindergarten and first grade and seemed to enjoy all school activities.

Test Results

Libby is a bright child, with a verbal WISC IQ score of 113, performance of 121, and full-scale of 119. No subtest score on either the WISC or the ITPA was below average, nor were there any deficits in visual or auditory perception. Deficits were evident, however, on the Frostig Movement Skills Test Battery. Libby had difficulties in crossing the midline of her body (block transfer), in bimanual coordination (bead stringing), and in arm strength (chair push-ups).

Achievement test scores were 3.5 in reading (one and one-half years above her age-grade level), 1.4 in spelling (six months below age grade level), and 2.2 in arithmetic (at about age-grade level). For a complete profile of Libby's test scores see Figure 9–4.

Observation revealed that Libby was a true mirror writer. She reversed each word completely. She showed poor letter formation. There often seemed to be general uncertainty in her gross movements. Motor performance was very variable. At times she had difficulty in throwing a bean bag, but not at other times. At times she could move around without mishaps; at other times she would fall. Her teacher complained about poor performance during gym and modern dance.

The remedial program for Libby focused on helping her to write without reversing letters and sounds. As reversals were consistent, it was concluded that Libby perceived two-dimensional figures as being positioned in the opposite direction in space. If this were the case, she would correctly reproduce a reversed figure. A slanted mirror was put behind the paper on which the teacher wrote a word. Libby was told to look at the writing in the mirror. Then the mirror was turned over so that it covered the writing, and Libby was told to copy what she had seen *in the mirror*. This method was successful; reversals dropped out in short order. After a few lessons Libby not only wrote correctly, but she also was actually unable to produce mirror writing.

Spelling was presented in a functional manner and integrated with writing skills. No specific method was used, for improvement was rapid. Words were written by the teacher, next they were analyzed phonetically and visually, and then Libby reproduced them from memory.

After four months of teaching the public school teacher reported that Libby did very well in her spelling tests and in writing.

Libby's handwriting is now legible but still not especially good. Letter formation has not improved sufficiently, and she has great difficulty in writing in a uniform size. She has been helped by using paper on which a colored stripe is drawn between the lines, to indicate the size of lower-case letters.

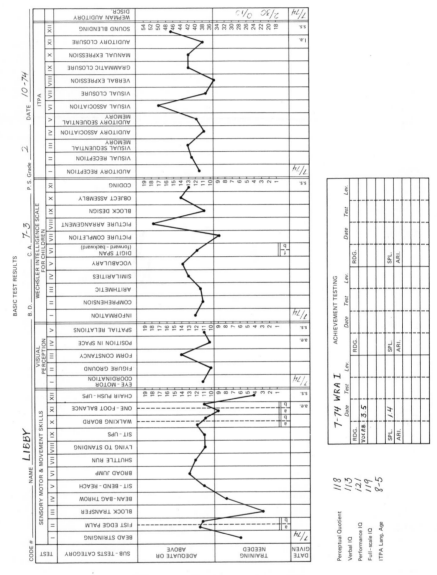

Fig. 9-4.   Basic test results: Libby.

However, the most important aspect of Libby's program has been the remedial training of motor functions. Exercises have been given for balance, crossing the midline, fine motor coordination, and muscle strength. There has been some improvement; Libby's retest score in bead stringing increased from 6 to 10 and in block transfer from 3 to 4. There has been no change in her chair push-ups score, probably because of her variability of performance.

Since Libby no longer had school difficulties, the number of her training sessions was reduced to one a week. She attended a class in modern dance and another in arts and crafts to improve her coordination further. Her tutoring sessions were terminated after about two months.

DARYL

His public school teacher referred 7-year-old Daryl for summer school. In her evaluation she stated that Daryl had visual–perceptual, auditory–perceptual, and sensorimotor difficulties and could not learn to read.

Daryl's birth and early motor development were normal. Speech developed slowly; his first words were probably spoken during his third year of life, though his mother is not sure about this. She does remember with certainty that his first sentences were spoken after his third birthday.

Daryl had frequent ear infections. His eardrum ruptured when he was 5 months old, and he suffered from recurring ear infections until he was about 5 years old.

Home Environment

Daryl's parents seemed to care greatly about him, without being overprotective or "overconcerned." There seemed to be no circumstances in his environment that might have contributed to his learning difficulties.

School History

Daryl attended nursery school for two years, from the time he was 3 years old until he was 5 years old. He did not like nursery school and had to be forced to attend.

He entered kindergarten at 5 years of age. There the children were introduced to prereading (letters and sounds). The teacher complained that Daryl could not learn any reading skills.

His first-grade teacher saw no progress in reading, and severe behavior problems occurred. Daryl upset the class by being noisy and by disturbing other children. Despite these signs of failure, the school did not consider retaining him in first grade.

Test Results

Audiological testing revealed that Daryl's hearing is slightly deficient. He has a low frequency loss in his right ear and a high frequency loss in his left ear. Visual acuity test results were normal.

Daryl's scores on the Frostig Movement Skills Test Battery were average or better (see Figure 9–5). The subtest scores in figure-ground perception and perception of position in space on the Frostig Developmental Test of Visual Perception were somewhat low (both with a scaled score of 8).

Daryl showed a discrepancy of 17 points in his scores on the WISC verbal and performance scales (verbal 97, performance 114, full-scale 106). Only one subtest score was low on the WISC, similarities. This score seemed to bear out his observed difficulty in comprehension of abstract material. Hearing comprehension tested with the Temple Word Recognition Inventory showed 70 percent comprehension at beginning second-grade level, 65 percent at beginning third-grade level, and zero comprehension at beginning fourth-grade level.

The ITPA indicated several deficiencies. His score on the visual sequential memory subtest was one year below age level; on auditory sequential memory, nearly three years below; on grammatic closure, one year; on auditory closure, one and one-half years; on sound blending, one and one-half years; and on visual association, a little over one year. The Wepman Test of Auditory Discrimination also showed some difficulties in discrimination of speech sounds in whole words.

The public school teacher had been correct in assuming that perceptual difficulties were instrumental in retarding Daryl's progress. However, formal test results and observations in the clinical setting failed to confirm her wories about Daryl's motor abilities.

Achievement test scores were at the first-grade level in all areas. Achievement test scores are not reliable at Daryl's low performance level, but observation showed that Daryl knew the sounds of only three letters, could read only three to five words, could not spell at all, and knew only a few number facts.

The teacher with whom Daryl worked during summer school decided to assist him with his socioemotional adjustment to the classroom situation before confronting him with reading. Daryl had a happy summer and his behavior improved greatly; but progress in reading and spelling was practically nil. Because of Daryl's improved attitude, the summer school teacher felt that Daryl would be able to make progress in public school provided he also received tutoring at the Frostig Center.

In the fall tutoring was begun on a twice-a-week basis. After two months Daryl's progress was evaluated. He could read quite well in a first-grade reader, but a beginning second-grade book was still too difficult for him. It was

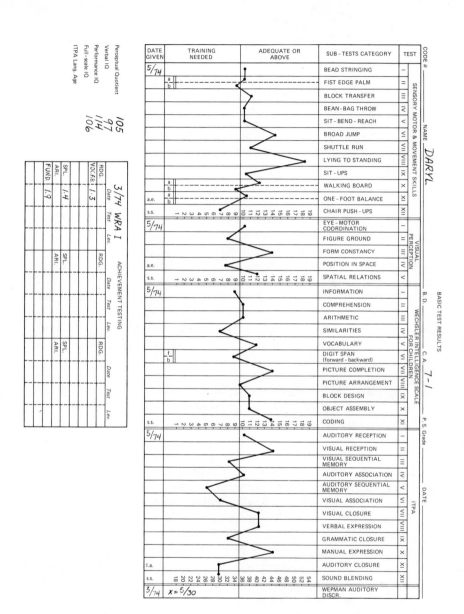

Fig. 9-5. Basic test results: Daryl.

felt that the length of time between tutoring sessions was too long, and tutoring was changed to three times a week.

Diagnosis and Prescription

Daryl had both auditory and visual perceptual deficits. The visual perceptual difficulties are evident in the subtest scores for figure-ground perception and perception of position in space of the Frostig Developmental Test of Visual Perception and for visual sequential memory of the ITPA. These deficits are relatively minor as compared with the auditory deficits but in children with auditory perceptual difficulties even minor visual perceptual disturbances may constitute a handicap because compensation becomes more difficult.

Daryl's lag in figure-ground perception was evident in reading. He had a good perception of the whole word, which might be expected from his high score in perception of form constancy, and when he finally learned to recognize a word, he could recognize it in different contexts and different prints. At first, however, he would look at one or a few letters and misread the word—for example, *scrap* for *script, tone* for *term,* and so on. He took some time to learn a word initially because of his poor memory for visual sequences. Much repetition was needed.

Because of difficulties in perception of position in space, Daryl could not readily differentiate between *b* and *d.* He would first write one of the letters and then decide which one it was. He had apparently memorized it kinesthetically. Visual perceptual training was done for a few minutes in each tutoring session, using one of the work sheets from *Pictures and Patterns* [10].

Daryl's greatest deficit was in auditory sequential memory, in which his score was nearly three years below his age level. With children who have both visual and auditory perceptual deficits, it is necessary to emphasize the modality in which the child has the better *sequential memory score,* even though the perceptual deficits may be greater in the other modality. Therefore, Daryl was taught reading by the whole-word method, which emphasizes the visual modality, despite his difficulties in visual perception.

Perceptually bound memory deficits are usually a greater detriment to learning to read than other perceptual skills. Jon Eisenson [11] is also of the opinion that a whole-word method must be used with children who have very poor auditory sequential memory in spite of visual perceptual deficits.

Auditory perceptual training for Daryl was limited. It started with training in perception of speech sounds and word boundaries—for example, "How many sounds do you hear in the word copy?" "How many words are there?" Children usually enjoy playing these games. The sentences that were given were very short at first but as time went on became progressively longer. When

Daryl could differentiate the sounds in words made up of three or four simple speech sounds, words containing digraphs, diphthongs, and blends were added. After these preliminary exercises, Daryl was asked to find words that the teacher pronounced on a page that she had printed. He also had to indicate by drawing slanted lines the separate sounds in the words—for example, *th/a/t*. Exercises in sound blending necessary for word synthesis were added to exercises for a clearer perception of speech sounds and the auditory analysis of words. The teacher wrote words for Daryl to read aloud, using a different color for each sound. When Daryl had read the word, it was written again in a single color for him to read. A flashcard was then made with the word written in a single color for purposes of review. Auditory memory is trained whenever a whole-word method is used, for the child has to remember the sound of the word.

Sequential memory in one modality was also practiced by having Daryl learn to say the days of the week and the names of the months (sequence), memorize number triads (number facts), and so on.

In addition, the following process was used to strengthen Daryl's auditory memory for words: the teacher read a page while Daryl looked on. Then Daryl and the teacher read the page together; after that Daryl read the page to the teacher. Words that had been difficult were written by Daryl and read again. Then Daryl and the teacher proceeded similarly with the next page. Afterward the teacher read the story into a tape recorder, and Daryl took his book and the tape recorder home to read the story again. He tried to keep ahead of his class so that he would be able to read aloud in school when asked to.

Daryl did not rebel against this cumbersome method because it helped him to succeed, at least to a degree. He no longer saw himself as a total failure, and seemingly no price was too high to pay for this. In January Daryl was able to read about 80 percent of the words in his book correctly without preparation. He had a reading vocabulary of several hundred words, but he was still unable to perform the simplest word analysis. He could not distinguish the two sounds in such two-letter words as *up* or *on*, for example. When asked what sounds he heard in *up*, he would answer with the word, *up*.

The teacher felt that the limit had been reached in what could be achieved by the use of only a visual method; it was necessary for Daryl to learn some phonics.

The teacher asked Daryl to write the consonant sounds that she pronounced *p-t-b-* and so on. Daryl could do this. He was then asked to listen for the difference between *p* alone and *p* with a short vowel—*pa*, for instance. The teacher then sounded the *a* and had Daryl reproduce it as well as the *p* sound. Daryl seemed confused if he was asked to join the letters.

A successful game was one in which the teacher pronounced a single consonant sound and Daryl wrote it in a box, followed by a consonant-vowel combination, followed by a consonant-vowel-consonant combination, each being written in the following manner

| t |

| t | a |

| t | a | g |

Daryl enjoyed "word building."

It is necesaary to use visual and kinesthetic cues to teach Daryl the short vowel sounds, and it is also necessary to invent many games to make the very difficult auditory tasks more pleasing. The addition of an auditory method accelerated Daryl's progress, and training in both auditory and visual perception was intensified. In the school year subsequent to summer school, Daryl progressed well in public school. Tutoring was continued for a while, however, as he was still slightly below his grade level.

KEVIN

In addition to continually evaluating a child's progress in basic academic skills and directly furthering his scholastic attainment, it is also necessary to note and respond to emotional factors that may interfere with progress and development. For Kevin, the subject of the present case history, these factors were taken into consideration. The strategy that resulted was to structure the classroom in such a way that he could comfortably take on the role of assistant.

Kevin had attended the Frostig Center in his eighth year. He had achieved age-adequate performance in each school subject, was considered ready for third grade in a regular school, and had returned there. At the end of the next school year his teacher remarked that Kevin was socially immature and withdrawn and that he seemed misplaced in the classroom. In class he would sit dreaming and sucking his thumb; he was often oblivious of his surroundings and did not complete the assigned tasks. The school psychologist who tested Kevin stated that he was up to grade level in all subjects and that he should continue in public school. Kevin's mother, however, was afraid that he would withdraw further into a world of dreams and asked that he be readmitted to the remedial school.

Kevin's behavior in the Frostig Center classroom was at first not much different than that described by his public school teacher. Academic achievement continued to be satisfactory. However, his work was done very slowly, and he often sat sucking his thumb and doing nothing else. Kevin was then transferred for one hour each day from a class of 12 children into a smaller class of 5 and given additional responsibilities. He was told to arrange science experiments for the whole class. He obtained the necessary materials with the help of the teacher. He was required to do these tasks with reasonable speed and good performance. Because of the new responsibility and position of leadership, as well as the continuous support from the teacher, Kevin's attitude and behavior changed for the better. He became a much more active, friendly, and self-assured participant in both his regular class and the smaller group.

GEORGE

The case histories of George and those of Margaret and Terry that follow are examples of counseling and supportive relating by teachers in a public school that served a rural and small town population. The children in the previous cases came from urban areas that had extensive supplementary psychological services available to their public school districts.

George, age 9, had recently moved to town with his mother. His report cards from the previous school showed only one mark, "unsatisfactory," in all areas of academic achievement and behavior.

On the day following George's enrollment in school, the classroom teacher was able to find out a great deal about George's feelings and attitudes from three drawings that he did and the descriptions that accompanied them.

1. This is a child in a boat. He does not know there is a waterfall. He will be swept down and his boat will turn over. He will drown.
2. This is lightning. There is a child. He will be hit and fall and slide down on the path. He will be dead.
3. In the picture there is a boy on a toboggan; he goes downhill. It is too steep; he will turn over.

The negative tone of the drawings and stories and the repeated connotations of accident and death suggested that George was depressed rather than hostile (as his class behavior seemed to indicate) and that his work and behavior were unsatisfactory as a result of his depression. What was the reason for his despair? What could the teacher do?

The teacher invited George's mother to school for an interview. During their talk the mother complained in a loud, whiny voice that her husband had had an operation because of cancer of the larynx. As a consequence, he was unable to speak, had been sitting at home, "of no use to anybody," and had finally left home. She pointed out that her life had been hard and that she had no money. The teacher responded by assuring the mother of her sympathy and her willingness to be helpful in any way possible.

At school the teacher made George feel welcome and wanted. She was successful in making him feel more competent, and this was reflected in his attitude and improvement in school work. She encouraged him to express himself through drawings, and she discussed his home situation with him, giving him verbal support and encouragement. At the same time she set definite standards of behavior that George, because he wished to please her, gradually learned to respect. The initial restlessness and destructiveness that George had displayed when he entered school diminished.

Soon after the school year ended George's father returned home. He had received help in a hospital and had learned to talk with an artificial larynx, although with a very changed voice. He had also received counseling in the hospital and felt better able to handle his affairs and get a job. George's later reports show that he continued at the school as a good and happy pupil.

The attitude of the teacher was decisive in this case in that she was supportive and respected the integrity of George and his mother. They felt valued and liked and responded positively in consequence. Any observation on the teacher's part that would have suggested a value judgment, such as "Your husband should really come back" or "You don't show enough understanding for your son," would have created havoc. The mother would have rejected immediately any idea of seeing a psychotherapist, even if one had been available. The mother felt injured and wronged, that life had dealt her a series of injustices; she did not feel emotionally disturbed. Her whining self-pity alienated people and prevented her from making friends. Indeed, her continuing contacts with the teacher seemed to be her only opportunity for expressing her feelings and of communicating with another adult. In order to manage at all, she needed interest and sympathy, which the teacher gave by being available and by listening.

To act as judge or to apply specific psychotherapeutic techniques is not the teacher's role. To help parents and children by giving support is always the teacher's responsibility.

In George's case the teacher assisted a child in a situation of crisis. In the following case she provided help that was probably instrumental in enabling a child to endure a situation that subsequently became critical.

MARGARET

Margaret was a child in the same class as George. Every day before school started she waited at the gate for her teacher. She often presented her with a flower or a letter. Every day she told the teacher how much she liked her and reported whatever she had done during the previous day that was of importance to her—for instance, that she had played with another child or had read a

Fig. 9-6. Young children often need the teacher's warmth and security to learn effectively. A teacher must be nurturant whenever the child shows a special need for attention. (Photo by James Quinn and Michael Campa.)

particular book. Nothing in her conversation or letters indicated why she had such a strong need to confide in the teacher. The teacher always thanked her for her notes and permitted Margaret to work in the room with her while she prepared for the children before or after school.

Once when the teacher asked Margaret if her parents would visit the class, Margaret said that her father had to travel a great deal and was rarely at home, while her mother had to stay indoors because she was sick. Margaret hoped that her mother would get well soon. She did not express her deep anxiety about her mother verbally, but the teacher then understood the child's needs better and continued to give her as much attention as possible.

A short time later Margaret's mother died. Margaret did not come to school, and the teacher heard of the event only after the funeral. Margaret was sent to live with relatives in another town, but the teacher was able to see her once more before she left. She consoled the crying child as best she could and promised to write to her. In the subsequent correspondence Margaret indicated that she eventually adjusted fairly well and found new friends.

This case, as was true for George too, illustrates how the teacher has to be available to the child whenever the child shows a special need for attention, even though the teacher may not understand the reason for the demand. Attention-getting behavior often arouses the teacher's anger or discomfort and is regarded as being ''bad.'' But attention-getting behavior indicates a need of the child, and the teacher should explore why the need exists and attempt to satisfy it. At the same time the teacher must take care to channel the satisfaction of the child's needs in such a way that there is no interference with the teacher's work, with the relationship of the teacher to other children, or with the work of the child and the other children.

TERRY

Terry, age 10, attended the same school as Margaret and George. In charge of his class was a young male teacher. Terry had been so unruly the year before that he had earned the nickname ''Terror.'' The teacher found out that Terry could play baseball very well for a child of his age. He made him captain of the team and sometimes let him be the coach without his supervision. Terry nearly burst with pride and took his responsibilities very seriously.

One day Terry arrived at school almost at the end of the school day. His face showed great anxiety. He said to the teacher, ''I'm sorry that I didn't come to school. My mother's out of town, and she left me at home with Karl [his year-old brother]. Karl's very sick. I'm afraid that he might die!'' The child was so anxious that the teacher himself went to see Karl, as no school nurse was available. He found that the children lived in a small, dirty mobile home on a vacant lot. Karl was covered with a rash and had a high fever. The teacher called a hospital, and Karl was taken to the hospital by an ambulance; he had scarlet fever. Terry stayed alone that night. On the following day his mother came home.

After these events Terry's behavior in class changed markedly for the better. He told the teacher: ''I want to be like you, you always help.'' The example illustrates how sometimes the teacher has to act as a neighborly human being and not only as an instructor.

SAM

There are unfortunately many cases in which the teacher can be of only limited help. The following is an example.

Sam, a thin, pale, 9-year-old boy who was unusually dirty and often covered with rashes lived with his parents and an older brother in a small trailer. The mother was a feeble, ailing woman who from time to time obtained some cleaning jobs. The father was an unskilled worker, whose working hours were ''swing shift,'' from one o'clock in the afternoon until midnight. Each night he brought home to the trailer a bottle of liquor and some friends, with whom he proceeded to have a party around the only table, in front of the bunk in which Sam and his brother slept. Each night the boys were awakened by the noise and kept awake until 3 A.M. or so, when the guests left and their father went to sleep. The older boy, Robert, was more able to take these circumstances in stride, but Sam usually could not go back to sleep. He became dead tired and often ill. He was too afraid of his father to make any complaint.

Once the mother visited the school and described a life of anxiety, submissiveness, and sickness. The father came twice to complain because Sam had been sent home due to a contagious rash.

There was no possibility of helping Sam to fulfill the wish he expressed in one of his compositions: "My greatest wish is to be able to sleep in the night without being waked up by the noisy men who come to the trailer." The teacher could only take into consideration the circumstances of Sam's life, relieve pressure as much as possible, and give him opportunities for rest as frequently as possible.

OTHER EXAMPLES OF CONSTRUCTIVE RESPONSES TO CHILDREN'S NEEDS

The principal of the school in which the above children were enrolled had fostered and encouraged the importance of guidance roles for his teachers. He himself was an excellent example. When a very deprived youngster stole a pair of roller skates, he made it possible for the child to receive a bicycle as a present for Christmas after the child had returned the skates. He realized that a bicycle could provide much of the joy, status, and mastery that this child needed. When another child had to repeat a grade, the principal restored his self-respect by appointing him to help another youngster with severe reading difficulties. He helped poverty-stricken Spanish-speaking migrant children to feel secure, accepted, and important by making their culture a major focus of instruction. He used instruction in sports and gymnastics to instill habits of self-control and self-discipline in the boys.

Pressures in the community often tend to force administrators and teachers to return to the "good old days," reinstitute regimentation and punishment, and adhere to strict group standards without making an allowance for individual differences. More repression leads to greater resistance, rebellion, and delinquency, while an approach that emphasizes mutual respect and explores the common problems of "authority figures" and the positive feelings of the children in relation to authority may prove to be most effective in terminating the vandalism and delinquencies that have made learning progress impossible in many schools.

To give an extreme example, two young students were killed at a school in

Fig. 9-7.   Older children need vigorous activity and a chance to compete in groups.
(Photo by James Quinn and Michael Campa.)

a very poor district in a suburb of Los Angeles. The police could not find any
clue to the murders. The assistant superintendent of this school district, an
unusually courageous man, was convinced that gang warfare had been the
cause of these crimes. He requested a meeting with boys whom he suspected to
be leaders of some of the gangs. At the meeting he stated his views that violence
as a method of settling grievances set a pattern that endangered the lives of
everybody and that he, therefore, wished to explore how such occurrences could
be prevented in the future. He did not want to punish anybody; his only goal
was prevention.

The discussion brought to light that the first murder occurred during one of
the usual gang "rumbles," while the second youngster—we shall call him
K.W.—had been killed by members of his own gang because of "insubordina-
tion." He had refused to wear the shirt that was a gang uniform in spite of
frequent warnings. The superintendent suggested finding out why K.W. had
shown such disloyalty. One boy reported that a discussion with K.W.'s parents
had indicated that they had been unable to give K.W. the necessary money to
buy the shirt. They were extremely poor; and whenever K.W. had occasionally
earned a few dollars, they had insisted on his contributing the money in
payment for his food. Being a child of religious parents, and with strong
religious feelings himself, K.W. had not dared to refuse or to lie or steal.

The superintendent confronted the suspected gang leaders with these

Fig. 9-8.   Young people benefit a great deal from earning their own money and from working together in a common enterprise. This group of younsters is earning money for a class trip. (Photo by James Quinn and Michael Campa.)

facts. They were horrified by what they had done and responded positively to the nonpunitive attitude of the educator, who kept his promise, gave no threat of punishment, and did not inquire as to who had committed the crime, but made the youngsters responsible for preventing any future misdeeds. The boys decided to atone as much as possible for their crime. They set up a car-wash business and turned over the money that they earned during the school year to K.W.'s parents. Certainly this was a small deed in payment for a human life, but it represented a change of attitude that may have saved many other lives. It also resulted in gangs conferring with each other instead of continuing their warfare.

The youngsters also continued their meetings with the superintendent, who assisted them in their new business, and listened to their grievances and anxieties concerning unemployment, drug addiction, other gangs, and so on. Slowly under his direction the gangs changed into clubs that were recognized by the school and that helped to channel the youngsters' energies into more legitimate outlets.

This superintendent was able to look beyond the immediate deed to evaluate various alternative courses of action in terms of long-range, community-wide effects. If he had ignored the well-documented fact that prisons and juvenile halls are schools for crime, he might have abdicated his responsibilities by breaking his word to the gang leaders and turning them over to the police. But he knew that punishment as such only increases antisocial behavior. He recognized instead that the group spirit and the great energies of the gang could be used for constructive as well as destructive purposes. In attempting to channel their energies constructively, he accepted the responsibility of an educator. It was his task to provide alternative positive courses of action, courses perceived by the gang members as both desirable and achievable. In short, he acted on the knowledge common to all successful youth workers that *delinquents must be redirected*.

This superintendent exemplifies the truly moral person as one who bases his actions on a system of values that transcends narrowly defined interests and groups.

REFERENCES

1. Farnham-Diggory S: Cognitive Synthesis in Negro and White Children, Monographs of the Society for Research in Child Development 35 (2 Serial No. 135), 1970
2. Orpet R: Frostig Movement Skills Test Battery (exp ed). Palo Alto, Calif., Consulting Psychologists Press, 1972
3. Kephart N: The Slow Learner in the Classroom (rev ed). Columbus, Ohio, Merrill, 1971
4. Frostig M: Move-Grow-Learn. Chicago, Follett, 1969
5. Kirk S A, McCarthy JJ, Kirk WD: The Illinois Test of Psycholinguistic Abilities (rev ed). Urbana, University of Illinois Press, 1968
6. Kirk S A: Illinois Test of Psycholinguistic Abilities: Its origins and implications, in Hellmuth J (ed): Learning Disorders, vol. 3. Seattle, Special Child Publications, 1968
7. Levi A: Treatment of a disorder of perception and concept formation in a case of school failure. J. Consult Psychol 29:289–295, 1965
8. Levi A. Remedial techniques in disorders of concept formation. J Spec Ed 1(1):3–8, 1966
9. Attribute Games and Problems. McGraw-Hill # 18479, 79896, 18480. Manchester, Missouri, Webster Division, McGraw-Hill, no date
10. Frostig M, Horne D, Miller A: Pictures and Patterns: Teacher's Guides and Workbooks (rev ed). Chicago, Follett, 1972
11. Eisenson J: Aphasia in Children. New York, Harper & Row, 1972

PART IV

Education for Social Change

Introduction

We have to help mankind to educate itself against the danger of its destroying itself; and this is a duty that we dare not repudiate.

Arnold Toynbee [1, p 37]

To this point in our examination of education in our time we have been concerned with the various aspects of education designed to prepare the child for adult life by providing him with information and skills, developing his abilities, and promoting harmonious emotional growth. This final section of the book discusses the child's moral education. It is concerned not only with the well-being of the child but with society as a whole.

The ethical principles that have provided moral guidance and the framework for our society for centuries now seem ineffective. Jacques Monod [2], a Nobel prize-winning biologist, has stated that current technological advances require not only a greater emphasis on ethical ground rules but also the development of a totally new ethics. Many other biologists agree with Monod that unless such ethics come into existence, the human race itself will not and cannot survive. It is already obvious to any sensitive person that, as Monod writes, the terrible destructive powers of present-day technology have endangered man's spiritual life [2, p 211]. The threats to his biological life increase daily. The many philosophers, scientists, and leaders of human destiny working in various fields who have expressed similar concerns have looked, and are looking, to education as the key for the future.

P. W. Musgrave [3] ascribes to the school an increasing role in moral education because the family's influence has decreased and the information on which moral decisions must be based has increased. The lesser influence of the family makes it necessary for another agency to take part in the child's moral education, and the accumulation of knowledge, especially technical knowledge, makes necessary more explicit teaching of the functional interrelationships and the consequences of various applications of that knowledge. Thus, the logical institution to assume a leading role in moral education is the school.

Chapter 10 explores the practical and ethical implications of two behavioral theories—those of Piaget and Skinner—that today are most influential in determining classroom methodologies and educational goals. Chapter 11 describes ways in which the school may affect the moral development of its students and, both directly and indirectly, the moral values of the society of which it is a part.

REFERENCES

1. Toynbee A; Education: The long view, in Black HC, Lottich KV, Seekinger DS (eds): The Great Educators, Chicago, Nelson-Hall, 1972, p 37
2. Monod J: Le hasard et la nécessité. Paris, Editions du Seuils, 1970
3. Musgrave PW: The Sociology of Education. London, Methuen, 1972

10

The Theories of Skinner and Piaget

. . . the point of education can be stated in behavioral terms: a teacher arranges contingencies under which the student acquires behavior which will be useful to him under other contingencies later on.

B. F. Skinner [1, p 184]

The principal goal of education is to create men who are capable of doing new things, not simply of repeating what other generations have done—men who are creative, inventive, and discoverers. The second goal of education is to form minds which can be critical, can verify, and not accept everything they are offered. The great danger today is of slogans, collective opinions, ready-made trends of thoughts. We have to be able to resist individually, to criticize, to distinguish between what is proven and what is not. So we need pupils who are active, who learn early to find out by themselves, partly by their own spontaneous activity and partly through material we set up for them; who learn early to tell what is verifiable and what is simply the first idea to come to them.

Jean Piaget [2, p 5]

Calls for a new ethics come from many sides, from philosophers, psychoanalysts, cognitive psychologists, biologists, and from people from all walks of life. Among the scientists, philosophers, and professional educators are some who not only sound the call but also provide us with signposts to direct us into the future. Some of these signposts may lead us into blind alleys; others may provide us with some foothold when the path becomes dangerous; others seem to indicate a direction that we can follow with some confidence if we wish to achieve our goals.

B. F. Skinner and Jean Piaget exemplify the contemporary psychologists who explore topics and methods that seem to have great import for any education that takes into account the future of mankind. Their work has already brought, and continues to bring, vast changes in education. Their books and articles, and the vast literature written about them, could fill a good-sized library. Education literature abounds with references to them and their work. It is mainly because of this overwhelming interest in their work that the author has chosen to discuss them in this chapter.

SKINNER AND BEHAVIOR MODIFICATION

B. F. Skinner has devoted himself to the development and refinement of a systematic application of techniques of behavior modification, derived from his research with animals. He has developed both a grandiose scheme for saving the world and a technology to achieve this purpose. His technology is widely used in education, psychotherapy, and industrial relations.

While behavior modification has been hailed by Skinner and his followers as the science that will deliver mankind from its dangers, some have totally condemned it and others find in it both virtues and vices. Some writers have attacked its basic philosophy as well as its specific applications, fearing that behavior modification may propagate a view of life and society in which the role of each individual is totally defined by outside forces. Such possible consequences have been described by Aldous Huxley [3], George Orwell [4], Anthony Burgess [5], Alvin Toffler [6], and others. In these writers' view behavioristic education may become a means of preparing a child to accept and contribute to a society that is rigidly controlled. D. McLean, for example, refers to behavorism as "a deadly enemy of the unfolding of an individual's creativity and an equally mortal threat to the future" [7, p 19]. Konrad Lorenz [8] includes behavioristic methods among the "eight deadly sins of mankind." Steven Forness and Don L. Macmillan [9] warn against the incorrect use of behavior modification in education.

At the other end of the critical spectrum are such authorities as Vitali Rozynko, Kenneth Swift, Josephine Swift, and Larney Boggs, who state,

> For the first time in the history of man we have acquired conceptual and technological tools that make it possible for us to control ourselves and others to the mutual benefit of society [10, pp 99–100].

It seems to this author that Rozynko and his associates may hope for too much, but they are only expressing the view of their master, B. F. Skinner, who has promised not only classrooms of orderly learning but also a world characterized by common happiness. There is, however, a cost—the abandonment of the tenets of freedom and dignity that are at the core of our present human and democratic ideals. Dignity is the experience of having worth. Can life be of value without it? Nevertheless, Skinner's ideas are influencing education enormously. This influence is being fed by the mounting disorder in our classrooms and some fear that there may be neither children nor teachers if the present course of disintegration in our society continues.

First we will discuss Skinner's suggestions to save mankind and then the application of his principles to classroom technology. Skinner states that contemporary society is supposed to be ruled by the fear of punishment but that punishment has not served to diminish crime, whether petty theft or wars, political killings, or mass murders. He points out that punishment increases anger against the punishing agency, which becomes regarded as an aggressor. John R. Platt quotes Skinner as stating that "this is why windows are broken in schools and not in drug stores" [11, p 29].

Since punishment has not worked as a deterrent, Skinner suggests that it be replaced by rewards for "good" behavior, that is, by operant conditioning. Skinner argues that if the consequences of behavior are pleasant, then these behaviors will occur more often. If positive reinforcement is given in the correct dosage and at the appropriate time intervals, then successive behaviors will be shaped until they assume the desired form, speed, frequency, and intensity.

Men have always tried to modify the behavior of others. After all, this is the purpose of education and the goal of all persuasion, whether the form be advertising, works of art, documentary reports, or child-rearing practices. All of these methods may be influential, especially if the same message is given repeatedly.

The essence of the technique of behavior modification is systematic reinforcement. Reinforcement as an educational method is not new. Attempts to modify human conduct by such means have played a significant part in every society since prehistoric times. In fact, the ability to learn through environmental contingencies is characteristic of all living species. Among the methods traditionally used in our own society for promoting behavior regarded as admirable are gifts, money, medals, chairmanships, applause, affection, praise, and plaques. They have not been used consistently, however. Only in our time has behavior modification been elevated to an applied science and reinforcement systematically adopted on a large scale to achieve specific results.

The Application of Skinner's Theories in the Classroom

Behavior modification in the classroom rests on Skinner's main observation that stimuli in the environment elicit behavior and that if stimuli are altered, behavior will also be modified. Behavior modification, therefore, consists of changing stimuli preceding or following behavior with the goal of changing the behavior itself. To give an example, a teacher may show a child a card that sets the arithmetic problem 2 + 4. The child answers 6, and the teacher smiles and says, "Good, John!" The card is the eliciting (preceding) stimulus, 6 is the response, and "Good, John!" is the stimulus following the response. Because the response 6 is followed by the stimulus "Good, John," it is more likely that John will say 6 the next time he is asked to add 2 and 4. "Good, John!" is, therefore, called the reinforcing stimulus.

Social reinforcers, such as a word of appreciation, a nod, or a smile, constitute a major portion of the teaching strategies of all good teachers. Any other form of acknowledgment of a child's satisfactory performance, such as stars or a good grade, will be greatly strengthened if it is accompanied by a sign of the teacher's personal satisfaction. Both the acknowledgment of the performance and the positive attention of the teacher or classmates are highly reinforcing to the child, especially if applied systematically.

Positive reinforcement thus has advantages over some conventional classroom practices—punishment, for example. Punishment (such as bad grades, scolding, staying after school, doing extra work, or physical abuse) is avoided because punishing behavior does not effect permanent change in a child's behavior. J. Kounin's observations in a natural environment indicated that neither warning nor scolding was effective [12].

Nevertheless, contrary to Skinner's principles, a few behaviorists (for example, Lovaas and his associates [13]) have proposed using aversive conditioning to stamp out severely maladaptive behavior, such as self-destructive activities. In aversive conditioning a noxious stimulus is used as long as the child or adult engages in behavior that is considered to be damaging or not helpful to himself or to others. The noxious stimulus ceases when the behavior ceases. For instance, an electric prod may be used whenever a child bites himself or hits at other children or retreats into pathological withdrawal; the current is turned off only when the behavior stops.

Aversive conditioning may be indicated as the treatment of last resort for severe long-standing pathology, but it certainly has no place in the classroom. It is only effective if the punishment is severe, but punishment necessarily has adverse side effects, tending to make the child anxious and mechanical in responses and destroying the child's creativity and joy in living.

Most behavior modifiers believe that unwanted or undesirable behavior should be ignored, for behavior that is not reinforced tends to become extinguished. This attitude too is open to question. Rather than always ignoring unwanted behavior, it is often better to redirect it. The teacher can provide the child with alternatives. Instead of saying, for example, "Don't scribble, Mary, that is awful writing," the teacher might say, "Mary, this paper has lines that show you the proper size of your letters. Try to write your next words touching these lines. If you write slower, the letters will look more uniform." And when Mary does better than before, the teacher will say, "Mary, that *is* an improvement! Do you see how these letters that touch the lines are bigger than those you wrote before and look much better?'' Or when John begins to wiggle in his seat, the teacher may say, ''John, would you mind coming here for a moment to clean the blackboard? It would be a great help.'' It is possible that the short interruption and the satisfaction of helping the teacher will enable John to complete his work to his and the teacher's satisfaction. Alternatively, a child who is teasing others or aimlessly walking around may be given a puzzle to work on, or asked to clean the erasers, or asked to help another child.

At times clarification of the child's feelings may improve the results of intervention. The teacher may say to a child who is upset because he has made a mistake, ''I think you are a bit angry because you made a mistake. How about correcting it with me? If you get another sheet of paper, we will make it right.'' Or, as happened in one instance, saying to a black child who taunted another black youngster because he made a mistake, ''He made you angry because you want all black people to be perfect. Why don't you help him find the correct answer?'' Redirecting a child in this way and clarifying his feelings as he searches for identity is more effective than simply putting a stop to unwanted behavior. The behaviorists are certainly correct, however, in their insistence on rewarding or acknowledging good behavior.

To systematize the giving of rewards, many teachers use charts. Each child has a chart on which performance is noted, either by a simple check mark or in the form of a graph that indicates the child's gains in classroom behavior and/or academic achievement. The check in itself probably has no value, but seeing one's own progress on a chart helps to convince a child whose ego development is poor that he or she is not only capable of improving performance, but is in fact doing it.

Tangible reinforcers may be needed in certain instances. These may consist of gifts given to the child after a satisfactory accomplishment or tokens that can later be exchanged for gifts or other rewards, such as play time or the permission to choose an activity. This procedure is called instituting a ''token economy,'' and the rewards are termed ''back-up reinforcers.'' The giving of tangible rewards is a legitimate educational procedure if practiced judiciously.

Sometimes the word ''contract'' is used for the arrangement made between teachers and children, but the term is not always justified. A contract is made among parties who have equal rights. If a child is told, ''You must do a certain number of examples, then you can go out and play,'' this can hardly be called a contract. Contracts can, however, be legitimate and beneficial, as in the case of Toni described later.

Programmed Instruction

In addition to providing children with reinforcements for approved behavior and employing classroom techniques designed to phase out unwanted behavior, behavior modifiers have also developed specific methods of instruction referred to as "programmed instruction."

In programmed instruction a book or teaching machine requires the student to respond to series of questions and to complete statements. Each question or statement is called a "frame" and is so constructed that the student acquires information in comprehending the question. Since the frames overlap (that is, in each frame a part of the statement of the previous frame is repeated), the cues for the responses are so apparent that mistakes can nearly always be avoided. The student himself checks if his answer is correct after completing a frame. In this way he receives immediate feedback, which is regarded as a form of reinforcement. Programmed instruction can be given either through the use of teaching machines or of programmed textbooks.

The advantages of programmed instruction are that it is self-correcting and that students can progress at their own rate and independently from the teacher. The disadvantages are that some students do not feel challenged and, therefore, are bored by the material and dislike it; and since in the vast majority of the programs only one answer to each frame is correct, the student follows the train of thought of somebody else so that original and divergent thinking is not possible.

Behavior Modification in the Classroom: A Critique

Many reports attest that the application of behavior-modification methods have resulted in accelerated progress for many children. Nevertheless, there are a number of valid reasons why many educators deplore the uncritical acceptance of the techniques as a panacea. These reasons include failure to take into consideration the child's moods and feelings; disregard of the student's intrinsic motivation and special interests; overemphasis on convergent thinking and neglect of divergent thinking; and the slow and invariant pace of much programmed material [7].

The most frequent mistake made by the more rigid behaviorists is probably neglecting to take the child's feelings into account. A child who is afraid because he has an appointment with the dentist after school or is upset because his parents have been arguing at home will react best to the teacher's reassurances and physical closeness. A programmed lesson does not give the child the opportunity to reveal these feelings to the teacher for there is not direct contact with the teacher during the lesson. The child who feels anxious because he is in a strange classroom may profit more from an explanation of the classroom rules by another child than from some tokens earned by completing his math problems, and the child who feels rambunctiously happy because she is invited to a birthday party may perform best if she is first given an opportunity to express her feelings and tell about the cause of her joy. In all such instances the understanding and acceptance of the child's feelings will result in far more than better work. It will also result in greater self-awareness on the child's part and a sense of a more deeply shared relationship with the teacher and the class. This has immense implications for a child's future happiness, fulfillment, and ability to care for others.

The second major disadvantage of behavior modification is the overemphasis on certain mental functions and the neglect of others. J. P. Guilford [14] has postulated that five different mental operations acting together constitute mental functioning—cognition, memory, convergent production (which leads to the one correct answer), divergent production (which produces many possible answers), and evaluation. Behaviorists emphasize convergent thinking, memory, and cognition, with evaluation playing a lesser role and divergent thinking being commonly neglected. Individual thinking and creativity are stifled by overemphasis on the "right answer." It is perhaps not surprising that the best results from behavior modification have been reported from work with the mentally retarded.

Nevertheless, many of the principles and techniques emphasized in behavior modification are of significant value in education, at least in respect to teaching skills and knowledge. They include (1) setting specific goals of learning for the student and letting the student know what the tasks will be to achieve these goals, (2) individualizing the student's program, (3) having each student start on a level at which he can succeed, (4) carefully analyzing the tasks presented to each child, (5) giving immediate feedback (knowledge of the correctness of the response), (6) proceeding in a careful step-by-step progression, and (7) systematically checking on progress and monitoring it through the use of written notes and graphs. Possibly more important than any other contribution to classroom management, however, is Skinner's suggestion that punishment should be avoided.

Even those procedures used by behaviorists that are judged to be unnecessary or harmful by some educators may be beneficial *if used judiciously at appropriate times*. For example, it may generally be regarded as preferable to encourage intrinsic motivation because it taps the child's natural pleasure in exploration and because it continues to induce learning when no external reward is available. Nevertheless, the previous examples have shown that extrinsic motivation has its value also, especially when a desirable learning pattern is not yet established and a child is resisting learning. In these cases resistance is usually lessened more quickly if extrinsic motivation is used.

Rewards should not be regarded as "bribes." Adults, including teachers, are paid for their work and do not regard payment as a bribe. For the child, the learning of multiplication tables is work too. As long as learning is not pleasant, rewards that make it more tolerable are certainly warranted. They can also contribute to the nurturing aspects of the classroom ecology.

To summarize, techniques of behavior modification do have a place in education, but they should never be used as the principal, or as the only, technique in classroom management. Overuse of the techniques can lead to the education of an overconforming, instead of self-directing, individual. It can also cause teachers to think and respond mechanically instead of creatively. Its value will depend on the teacher's goals.

Much of the technology of behavior modification has changed since its first inception. For instance, teaching machines and the giving of tangible reinforcers (candy, trinkets, and so on) are used much less frequently. Techniques of behavior modification other than positive reinforcement are emphasized—such as modeling, which is so important in all education. Unfortunately, despite Skinner's suggestion to the contrary, there still exists the use of punishment, both in the form of aversive conditioning and of more old-fashioned methods.

Techniques of behavior modification for exceptional children are discussed lucidly in F. Hewett and S. Forness' book, *Education of Exceptional Learners* [15], a book that reflects the change of these techniques used in the classroom, especially those Hewett introduced himself.

The enormous acceptance of behavior modification in the classroom indicates that classroom management is made easier for many teachers by the use of techniques of classroom management suggested by Skinner and his followers. However, educational journals and books concerning behavior modification in the classroom fail to indicate any connection between Skinner's methods of classroom management and the emergence of his design for a new society. The behaviors that the teacher attempts to change by Skinnerian methods are important for the acquisition of school learning—for example, staying with a task, giving undivided attention, and following promptly the teacher's suggestions. But the vast literature on behavior modification in the classroom does not indicate how any understanding of worldwide problems can be achieved or attitudes of genuine empathy acquired via behavior modification. It seems that the methods suggested may be effective in educating followers, but followers of what? The quality of many of the world's leaders, past and present, suggests that masses who merely follow may end up like the rats following the Pied Piper of Hamlin. It seems dangerous to develop behavior that is externally motivated rather than rooted in supple intelligence combined with a deeply felt morality.

Behavior Modification Modified: The Giving of Gifts

All children, especially economically deprived children, may be immensely gratified by receiving a gift from a person with whom a significant and caring relationship has been developed. Children who are anxious and restless because they are deprived of love and attention may also be greatly relieved by the frequent provision of small tangible rewards that provide symbolic restitution and also signify that the teacher is attentive. They will only be effective, however, if the child feels that the teacher genuinely cares and is not merely a dispensing machine. Subsequently, the tangible rewards can and should be replaced by such social reinforcers as a smile, a nod, or physical contact (which should be equally genuine).

The anthropologist Marcel Mauss [16] has shown that the giving of gifts holds groups and individuals together. It is a universal phenomenon that permeates the customs of all societies. Gifts have both a material and a symbolic meaning. A poverty-stricken ghetto child may be rapturously happy because he is given a toy when he has so few, if any; the child who has everything might be most deeply touched and provided with a peak experience because a gift symbolizes a teacher's love [17]. Behaviorists tend to ignore the symbolic meaning, while psychoanalysts sometimes forget the material value.

The following example illustrates the value of providing reinforcement in circumstances that justify the procedure. It was attempted in a classroom in which behavior modification is not habitually used, nor dispensed according to a carefully worked-out reinforcement schedule. In this classroom the tangible gifts were the exceptions, given individually according to the child's needs. Reinforcement schedules were used only in very exceptional cases, and then only for a limited period.

Larry, and his twin brother Lester, 6 years old, were referred to the Marianne Frostig Center of Educational Therapy, because their extreme hyperactivity and social immaturity had made it impossible for them to regulate their behavior and to learn in the setting of a regular school. They had been adopted a few months previously, and within three weeks of the adoption their adoptive mother had suddenly left the home. Prior to their adoption they had not received any consistent treatment, either in terms of understanding and affection or of discipline from the various adults with whom they had come in contact. They now had the security of a permanent home and material possessions and comforts, but they were still deprived of affective satisfactions and social guidance and modeling. When their adoptive mother left, the restlessness of the twins became much worse. Both children were compulsive talkers, noisy, and in continuous motion all day long. Under the comforting influence of an attentive teacher and flexible classroom environment at the Center, Lester calmed down considerably, but Larry continued to try to run around the school seeking continuous attention from any and all adults but refusing to follow his teacher's directions and doing little work. His teacher finally decided to work with Larry for 20 minutes daily on an individual basis in addition to providing continuous social reinforcers of personal attention and approval, with frequent body contact. She sat very close to Larry, and whenever he responded correctly in attempting work, behaved in a controlled way, or interacted appropriately with other children, she offered some food in the form of cereal or raisins. Through this approach Larry gradually learned to control his impulsive behavior. As his behavior improved, the teacher was able to reduce the number of rewards, eventually providing only occasional presents. When Larry was able to maintain attention quite consistently, the gifts and the individual lessons were stopped without ill effect. Larry is still somewhat hyperactive but to nothing like the previous degree. If he seems to feel restless, the teacher will permit him to move around for a minute or two, and he is then usually able to resume his seat and his task.

In Larry's case a reinforcement schedule was used, though only for a relatively brief period, but it is essential to understand that these behavior control techniques were only part of the total effort to help Larry's growth. He was part of a class in which the emotional needs of the children as well as their learning difficulties were taken into account; he had regular supportive therapy sessions with a warm and loving adult; and attempts were made (with minimal success in this instance) to guide the father and household staff in handling the children more adequately and consistently. In the long run Larry's treatment was successful because of the overall care and concern that he experienced, of which the behavior modification program was a temporary and most helpful expression.

The following examples of Toni and Leo illustrate the importance of the symbolic meaning of a gift.

Toni, an overweight 9-year-old girl, lives in a poverty-stricken neighborhood. She did not respond to small presents; she did not seem to cherish trinkets; and food provided no incentive. She seemed always to be able to get small amounts of money from somebody—her mother or a neighbor—which resulted in her being the best customer of the candy machine.

Toni's parents were divorced, and she only rarely saw her father, who is ill and out of work. Her mother worked on swing shift and often during the night so that Toni was alone at home much of the time. Sometimes the mother left town altogether for a few days, putting Toni in charge of the house.

Toni was large and tall for her age. When she entered the school, her manner was authoritarian, and she was determined to do exactly what she wished, which rarely included the performance of a learning task. She upset the teacher and the other children with her boisterous, bellicose, nonconforming, and impolite behavior. One of the difficulties Toni posed was that she often came to school an hour or more late; sometimes she did not come at all.

In spite of her evident hostility, Toni seemed to like the teacher who worked mainly with her. Although her responses were always unpredictable, she often followed directions without pouting or sighing, and when she had the freedom to choose her activity, she invariably joined the group with which that particular teacher was working. The teacher was deeply concerned about her. She understood that Toni's boisterous, bossy, and irritating behavior and refusal to learn reflected her attempt to prove to herself that she was the master of her own domain in the tough world in which she was forced to fend for herself.

One day the teacher did not come to school because she had been in a severe car accident. The children were told that she was in the hospital and would not be returning for some time. Toni showed the depth of her concern by continuously asking about her.

The injured teacher was equally worried about Toni. She was afraid that Toni might stay out of school and spend her time on the street while she was away. She sent a message to Toni telling her that she would send her a Mickey Mouse watch that she owned provided that Toni arrived at school on time each day for a month. She would have to show that she could use a clock by using her mother's alarm clock to wake herself up each morning.

The replacement teacher in Toni's class gave her a calendar on which to cross off each day so that she could see her progress toward her goal, and it was agreed that five extra days of punctual attendance would be required for every time she was late. To everyone's astonishment, Toni's attendance was impeccable. She earned the watch in a month and assured her substitute teacher that she would continue to come on time. In fact, she now frequently arrived up to an hour early.

Clearly, in this instance, the present from someone important to her motivated Toni to concentrate on establishing a routine because it constituted a symbol of the teacher's regard for her. As a result, Toni found herself enjoying greater success in school and in her relationships with other children. This, in turn, helped her to begin to trust her teachers and to be willing to try harder to please them. The original teacher had become a pattern of the "good parent," and Toni wished to be like her.

The example is not typical of a behavior-modification program, which would entail specific management for a period of weeks or months. Behavior is generally shaped or changed slowly, and reinforcement can be eliminated only gradually. In this case Toni was responding not to planned reinforcement but to an act of love and generosity, which was not the less because the teacher asked Toni to do something that would be of benefit to her. Later reinforcement flowed naturally from the greater acceptance by the group, the successes in learning, and the constant love of the teacher. The modification of Toni's behavior, therefore, resulted from a single experience of intense gratification followed by continuous reinforcement through a school situation of which she had previously not been able to take full advantage.

The case of Leo, which follows, illustrates that reinforcement can occur without the teacher's awareness, and as a result an inadvertent suspension of the reinforcement may occur with unfortunate consequences. Teachers need to watch carefully the ways in which children are reinforced during the course of the school day so they can take advantage of positive results and avoid mishaps.

Leo is a 12-year-old boy who lives, like Toni, in a poor neighborhood. There is no father in the family. Leo had been diagnosed as suffering from learning disability and had been excluded from public school. He was a very poor reader and had difficulties in other academic subjects, but he showed no gross behavior disturbances.

The learning that he seemed to enjoy most was math, but one day when his teacher gave him a sheet of examples to complete, he became extremely upset, began to cry, and astonished his teacher by accusing her of injustice, of hating him, and of not keeping her word. When his outburst had subsided, the teacher discovered that he had become upset because she had always provided Leo with preliminary training with three-dimensional materials before assigning pencil-and-paper math tasks, but on this occasion she had neglected to do so. She found that Leo had regarded math materials as his "toys." Most of the other children had toys at home; he did not—and on this occasion he had been deprived of his "toys" at school. The teacher took care from then on to provide Leo with some extra "math play" time and arranged some gifts of toys for him at Christmas and on his birthday through a charitable organization.

PIAGET'S THEORIES AND THEIR IMPLICATIONS FOR EDUCATION

Jean Piaget, whose influence in education and psychological circles is still in the ascent, has not set up any grandiose scheme to change our society, but his contributions have provided the educator with new insights in regard to the development of cognition and to its possible enhancement. Another of Piaget's many scientific explorations of utmost interest to the educator is his study of the development of morality [18]. Both of these aspects of his research are important for the educator because the predicament in which humanity currently finds itself can be traced both to an insufficient ability to plan and solve common problems and to an unstable as well as a materialistic morality.

Cognitive Development

Piaget's findings in regard to the child's cognitive development and their implication for education will be discussed first. The word *cognition* is often understood as pertaining only to thought processes. In this book the term is used as Piaget uses it—to denote the processes by which the environment is perceived and becomes known, whether these processes involve the use of motor or perceptual skills, language, or thought. In an article titled "Piaget Rediscovered"* Eleanor Duckworth [19] discusses in a few pages some of Piaget's suggestions for the education of cognition. She states that the main features of a cognitive education based on Piaget's work are that children are allowed their own learning, that the subject matter presented should be unified (also emphasized by Bruner and by many other cognitive psychologists as well as behaviorists), that all learning should result from the child's activity, and that the child, therefore, should have ample opportunity to experiment and view the results of his own actions.

More detailed suggestions for the application of Piaget's ideas to education can be deduced from his explanation of the characteristics of the child's intellectual development. Piaget posits four factors that influence the changes in the child's intellectual capabilities during his formative years:

*This title underscores the fact that the master's early fame had faded before he once more became "fashionable" and one of the guiding stars in education.

1. The effects of heredity and internal maturation—which cannot be separated from those that result from experience and learning.
2. Physical experience—the action of the child on objects.
3. Social transmission—education in the widest sense.
4. Equilibrium—the motivating force in Piaget's theory, and the most important of the four factors. The organism seeks to bring about a balance of assimilation and accommodation, the two processes that are complementary.

Piaget uses the term *assimilation* to refer to a process by which the mind "grasps" events and the person tries to incorporate them into the fund of his experiences. All experience must be adapted to particular situations to be used adequately. For instance, a child who has learned to write with a pencil but then is given a pen has to adapt his writing skills to the pen. This process Piaget terms *accommodation*. Assimilation and accommodation interact until a new equilibrium is reached [see 20, pp 88ff]. The teacher can successfully teach only that which can be assimilated and to which the child can accommodate.

Piaget points out that the equilibration process that guides the child in development obtains its driving energy from a child's *need* for equilibration. The child *wants* to know how to ride a bicycle, to learn about other countries, to master the skill of drawing a person, and in general to expand his knowledge and range of skills. Exerting effort is necessary in this process. S. H. Lawrence and L. Festinger's research [21] showed that effort is necessary for optimum learning and remembering. The sentence "A child should be challenged but not pressured" acquires additional meaning in the light of Piaget's research. It suggests that the child should be presented with an optimum amount of new learning but never with something for which he has not developed the necessary structures to assimilate it. The optimum cognitive development is only possible when (1) the child is routinely engaged in tasks for which he is developmentally ready, (2) he is stimulated by situations conducive to learning (a pen is available to him, to take the foregoing example), and (3) he exerts effort. Equilibration is not an automatic process; it depends on the child's activities, explorations, and self-direction. The child has to try to find out by himself. From Piaget's interpretations of his observations of the growing child, the teacher can conclude that the intellectual development of the child will depend to a considerable extent on his experiences in the situations provided for him.

Piaget's theoretical considerations also permit us to draw conclusions regarding the preparation of a child for academic learning. The child is required in school to solve problems through thought—but thinking requires many abilities, including the ability to classify, to seriate, to compare, to place in correspondence, and to sort according to multiple criteria. Before these functions can be mastered by thought processes, they have to be solved by action. Piaget terms this phase of development, in which thought processes must stem from concrete situations, "the phase of concrete operations." The child has to observe in order to master a problem.

Long before Piaget's discoveries could serve as an underpinning for her methods, Maria Montessori [22] was aware of the connection between action and thought and developed her materials to prepare and assist the child's learning. Although the insights of both Montessori and Piaget should guide the educator safely in monitoring each child's school progress, use of activities as preparation for schoolwork is often neglected, leaving children faced with academic tasks without the necessary prior experience and learning. Piaget has shown that all children pass through the same stages during their development, but children may differ in the chronological age at which they enter a given stage, depending on both hereditary and environmental factors.

Nevertheless, although the tempo is not uniform, the sequence of the developmental stages remains the same, as confirmed by the findings of C. Boisclar and A. Pinnard [23,24] among others. These workers compared the intellectual development of children in Switzerland, Rwanda, Canada, and Martinique. They found that when children engage in manifold activities and play together, arguing, solving problems, and making playthings, they develop faster than children who do not engage in activities and social interaction. On the

Fig. 10-1. Manipulation of three-dimensional materials combined with symbolic notation make learning arithmetic easier and more enjoyable. The child is actively engaged in learning. (Photo by James Quinn and Michael Campa.)

other hand, when children who were deprived of activities and of opportunities for playing together were placed in a traditional school, their development was not accelerated. These observations suggest that a classroom in which literacy skills are passively acquired by the child will not further his cognitive development as much as one in which social contacts, explorative learning, and play are stressed. These elements are important during both the preschool and the elementary school years, with the difference that the young child solves problems through physical action and the older child uses symbolism and speech, mental pictures and mental manipulation.* The child's intellectual development can be furthered by enhancing his symbolic or representational processes —language, imagery, and deferred imitation.

Piaget's research in cognitive development has radically influenced educational practices, notably affecting the teaching of mathematics and science, changing the approach to these subjects from mere book learning to experimentation and observation. Playgrounds, activity groups, and, for the older child, discussion groups are important adjuncts to book learning.

As has been mentioned, during a considerable part of the child's life play is at least as important for the equilibration process as academic learning. This fact applies to the child's social and emotional as well as his cognitive development. In imaginative play the child assimilates his feelings as well as his knowledge.

Children with learning difficulties are often unable to play. Their activities on the playground frequently consist merely of motor exercise, running without purpose, throwing, and pushing and hitting. These children have to be taught to play. For many teachers in conservative and traditional schools this is a new task.

A Critique of the Piagetian Approach to Education

Cognitive psychology has contributed greatly to our educational procedures. Piaget has been most influential in bringing about classroom structures that are less dominated by the teacher and that give the child more freedom to explore.

Piaget's observations of children contradict Skinner's opinion that observing pigeons can teach us how to educate children, especially where a new ethics is concerned. Skinner's poor pigeons have little ability to plan—and little time to do so if they could. Piaget has respect for the difficulty that the child faces in learning about the environment, in understanding it, in adjusting to it, and in developing the ability to judge, weigh decisions, and plan. Yet Piaget warns us

---

*In mental manipulation physical movement is replaced by mentally rearranging the terms of a problem. An example would be rearranging the terms of an equation. Mental manipulation is interiorized action.

not to interfere too much; rather we should give the child opportunities to learn by himself, to choose his own activities, to make his own responses to materials, and to interact with other children.

Piaget's theories of child development, of the sensory origin of knowledge, and of the importance of play, his methods of conducting observations and research, and his research and conclusions on a host of other topics give many suggestions to the educator. They cannot, however, be regarded as a complete guide to education. Although Piaget recognizes the importance of education, he gives little direct advice to the teacher on how to be more effective, nor does he discuss situations or materials with which the child might be presented to stimulate him to find out about the world around him. On the other hand, Piaget's findings can give direction to education so that a program can be developed to guide the cognitive development of the children effectively. Both the Compton and the Hartford programs, detailed earlier, could not have existed in the described form without the findings of Piaget.

Although Piaget has formulated no overall plan to reform society, he has heightened our understanding of the relationship of intelligence to moral conduct and thus erected an important guidepost for the educator.

Much of the evil in this world is not caused by ill will but by inability to plan and to assess all possible consequences. No one foresaw, for example, that thousands of Japanese would become ill, be crippled, and die because of mercury released in the ocean by industry. It seems that the more people interfere with nature, the greater are the difficulties that arise. Short-term gains are often paid for by long-term losses. The ill effects of thoughtless interference are seen all over the world. By teaching the child to plan for and with others, with his classmates, with the child that he tutors, with friends, with whomever he is engaged in recreational activities, he may develop the necessary attitudes and abilities to plan later on a bigger scale.

CONCLUSION

Piaget and the cognitive psychologists and Skinner and the behavior modifiers have many followers—students, adherents, and admirers. The research of both Piaget and Skinner suggests methods that can be applied in the classroom. Many of the suggestions can be combined, but there are also unbridgable chasms between important aspects of their theories and models. Piaget believes in the child's intrinsic joy in learning, Skinner in extrinsic motivation. Some of Skinner's followers, such as Hewett and Forness [15], concede that intrinsic motivation exists, but they still believe that this is a rarity and a stage difficult to reach. Good teachers, however, know that motivation, joy, and excitement in learning depend on the teacher's teaching techniques and classroom atmosphere. This author has worked for many years with both exceptional and so-called "normal" children, with both the well-behaved and the delinquents, and it was the exception rather than the rule for a child, regardless of his "classification," not to feel joy in exploring and learning about new things.

It is true that practice and review are not always rewarding. Then extra encouragement is not only helpful but often necessary to insure sufficient effort. Such encouragement may be given in the form of praise, pictorial or graphical representations of the child's accomplishments (such as a graph representing the number of pages read), or even in a promise of a pleasurable activity or gift.

The human beings whom Piaget and Skinner envisage as being able to enjoy life most fully seem to be quite different. Skinner's "happy person of the future" is a passive follower, while Piaget's is an active, exploring, creating human being. But who will be the leaders, and how will they be chosen and educated? Skinner does not answer these questions to this writer's satisfaction.

In this author's opinion Skinner's ideas can contribute to education, but they are not new. Piaget's ideas are also anchored in the past. It has been rightly noted that "the progressive education movement has proposed similar principles for many years" [25]. In fact, Dewey's educational ideas [26] were essentially the same. There is also a kinship with Montessori. Learning by doing and being self-reliant are the main tenets of Dewey, Montessori and Piaget alike.

The history of education is replete with forgotten and neglected teachings of great educators. Some are later resurrected, but more often than not their teachings become distorted by their followers. Some of Montessori's ideas became popular about thirty years after her death, and Dewey's are now arousing new interest. A teacher who is not thoroughly knowledgeable about the work of these leaders and unable to apply their findings in the classroom is poorly prepared.

One can conclude that barriers to achieving a new ethics are in part the result of inadequate teacher education. Teachers, at least in the United States, do not always read as much or as critically as they should, do not compare and integrate what they read, and do not apply it to classroom practice. A reason often given is that boards of education are formed of lay people who often do not understand education but greatly influence it. There is much truth in these pronouncements. The boards have powers of hiring and firing, and superintendents of schools are frequently changed, as are the philosophies that dominate a school system. Nevertheless, there is usually enough freedom to choose one's curriculum and the activities within it to achieve one's purposes. School boards can often be persuaded to listen to the educators when they feel pride in the achievement of the children. But when a stultifying curriculum of skills, and nothing but skills, grammatic rules, phonic rules, calculation, and the like, is required, then children and teacher will become miserable and finally hostile. Then there is no hope for education to improve the quality of life of the children or to influence the quality of life in the future.

REFERENCES

1. Skinner BF: About Behaviorism. New York, Knopf, 1974
2. Piaget J: In Ripple RE and Rockcastle VN (eds): Piaget Rediscovered. Ithaca NY, Cornell University, 1964
3. Huxley A: Brave New World. New York, Harper & Row, 1932
4. Orwell G: Nineteen Eighty-Four. New York, New American Library, 1971
5. Burgess A: Clockwork Orange. New York, Norton, 1963
6. Toffler A: Future Shock. New York, Random House, 1970
7. McLean D (ed): It's People That Matter. Sydney, Austral., Angus & Robertson, 1969
8. Lorenz K: Die Acht Todsunden der Zivilisierten Manschheit. Munich, Piper, 1973
9. Forness S, Macmillan DL: Reinforcement overkill: Implications for education of the retarded. J Spec Ed 6:221–230, 1972
10. Rozynko V, Swift K, Swift J, Boggs L: Controlled environments for social change, in Wheeler H (ed): Beyond the Punitive Society. San Francisco, Freeman, 1973
11. Platt JR: The Skinnerian revolution, in Wheeler H (ed: Beyond the Punitive Society. San Francisco, Freeman, 1973
12. Kounin J: Unpublished lecture presented at the meeting of the American Psychological Association, New York, 1966
13. Lovaas OI et al: Experimental studies in childhood schizophrenia: III. Developing social behaviors using electric shock. J Exp Res Personality 1:99–109, 1965
14. Guilford JP: The Nature of Human Intelligence. New York, McGraw-Hill, 1967
15. Hewett F, Forness S: Education of Exceptional Learners. Boston, Allyn & Bacon, 1974
16. Mauss M: Sociologie et anthropologie. Paris, Université de France, 1950
17. Maslow AH: Lessons from the peak-experiences. J Human Psychol 17:9–18, 1962
18. Piaget J: The Moral Judgement of the Child. London, Routledge and Kegan Paul, 1932
19. Duckworth E: Piaget rediscovered. J Res Sci Teaching 2:3, 1964
20. Frostig M, Maslow P: Learning Problems in the Classroom. New York, Grune & Stratton, 1973
21. Lawrence DH, Festinger L: Deterrents and Reinforcement: The Psychology of the Insufficient Reward. Palo Alto, Calif., Stanford University Press, 1962
22. Montessori M: The Montessori Method. New York, Schocken, 1964
23. Boisclair C, Dubreuil G: La pensée précausale chez un groupe d'enfants martiniquais, in Benoist J (ed): Montréal, Centre de Recherches Caraibes, Université de Montréal
24. Pinard A, Lavoie G: Perception and conservation of length: Comparative study of Rwandese and French-Canadian children. Perceptual and Motor Skills 39:363–368, 1974

25. Ginsburg H, Opper S: Piaget's Theory of Intellectual Development: An Introduction. Englewood Cliffs, N.J., Prentice-Hall, 1969
26. Dewey J: Experience and Education. New York, Collier, 1938

11
The Role of the School
in Moral Education

. . . the only happiness that is lasting: to increase, by whatever is yours to give, the good will and the higher order in your sector of the world.
Erik Erikson [1, p 124]

As the potentiality for both the good and evil of technology increases in our times, a stronger and deeper commitment to moral principles is needed. It is the author's belief that it is the school who should be in the forefront in bringing about this commitment. Some of the steps that teachers and other educational personnel may take to bring about a new moral commitment of society as a whole will therefore be discussed in this chapter.

These steps are typically rather small, each insignificant by itself, but together they can be important. We must have the insight, the will, and the courage to take these steps. Our work with children and with our colleagues provides many opportunities for influencing the children who will weave the carpet of the future. Our influence may be either positive or negative. We must take positive steps—at the same time we must avoid mistakes.*

The first step the teacher must take is to make a conscious, explicit, strong commitment to influence the moral standards of the children in his or her care. The second step is to become aware of what such an undertaking demands.

For this purpose, the teacher must first define the terms *moral* and *ethical*.

---

*Many books have been written picturing the potential damage that can be caused by the school, especially in relation to minority groups. One of these careful studies is by Charles E. Silberman, *Crisis in the Classroom* [2]

The words *ethical* and *moral* are here used interchangeably.** *Ethical* is used by philosophers to denote a system of values. At the center of this system is the attitude of not wanting to harm others, to love one's neighbor as oneself, often called the Golden Rule. By extension, this rule implies that one must take into account all present and foreseeable future conditions and strive to provide for future generations, if not for this one, what "ought to be."

John Platt stated, "The only power in the world that moves men to large efforts is the gap between what is and what might be" [3, p 49]. Human beings seem to be able to achieve miracles if they work with the hope for a better future.

Jacques Monod [4] states that no system of values can be called ethical if it does not include at least one ideal that so transcends the self-interest of the individual that he will be willing to sacrifice his life for it. We can hardly regard this attitude as a goal of public school education, but we certainly can go so far as to teach children that each individual has to make some sacrifices for one's own ideals and to assure a happy and safe future for one's fellow men. The limits to which a person is willing to make sacrifices are up to that individual.

COGNITIVE AND MORAL DEVELOPMENT

Children as young as 3 years are capable of predicting what other children will feel in a familiar situation, such as eating dessert, losing a toy, and so on [5]. The author remembers her daughter at the age of 2 years and 9 months imploring the driver of a car to stop during a pelting rain to take some cows standing on a distant meadow into the car so that the poor cows would not get so wet. Even when the impossibility of granting the request has to be patiently explained, expressions of empathy should be encouraged and nurtured. There is no doubt that affective components of morality can be influenced at an early age [6].

The young child, however, is not capable of flexible empathy, that is, "the ability to predict, keep distinct, and yet simultaneously relate the different viewpoints of others to objectively the *same* external event(s)" [7, p 281]. Flexible empathy is practically nonexistent in preschool children and is still developing in adolescence [8, 9]. It requires the ability to understand the perceptions and viewpoints of others (in Piaget's term, to "decenter"—see p 14). and to understand logical relationships, particularly that of reciprocity.

Piaget [10] has traced the moral as well as the cognitive development of the child through distinct phases. In the beginning the young child respects orders only when the person who gave them is present, but later the child is able to

**Educators and other professional people often use "ethical" and "unethical" to connote adherence to or breach of a professional code. When used in this restricted sense, "ethical" behavior may contradict "moral" behavior.

identify with the authority figure and to obey rules even when that figure is not present. Freud refers to this as the formation of the superego. The child develops the opinion that given rules should direct behavior independent of the validity of the rule or of the circumstances in which it is applied. This is called the stage of moral realism, and it requires "objective responsibility," by which Piaget means that a person at this stage of development does not take into account any other person's intentions or reasons for transgressing a law but only judges as important the degree to which he has transgressed it. A transgression should be punished in the same way whatever the circumstances in which it took place or the motives of the transgressor.

Later the child enters what Freud calls the latency stage; Piaget, the stage of concrete operations. The child becomes able to see the purpose of rules and strives to establish and change them by mutual consent.

In the third stage, the child can understand that intentions, consequences for society, and factors that caused the deed should also be taken into consideration. This stage is called by Piaget the "stage of equity."

Many people unfortunately never proceed to a higher moral level than moral realism. Especially when anxiety rises in times of great stress, the cry of "a tooth for a tooth" is heard loudly, the thirst for revenge requires punishment whatever the circumstances of the misdeed, and even capital punishment becomes widely acclaimed.

There is no doubt that intellectual maturity is a precondition for mature moral judgment. Lawrence Kohlberg and his associates have presented and tested a model of moral development that explicitly states that higher levels of cognitive development must be attained before higher, more mature levels of moral judgment can be reached [11]. William Damon has related the development of a child's conception of justice to Piaget's operational stages, classification behavior, compensation behavior, and perspective taking [12].

Although cognitive development is a necessary condition, it is not sufficient by itself to insure moral development. Moral judgment and behavior require the interrelationships of both cognitive and affective factors—knowledge and understanding and social and emotional development. The vehicles for moral education in the classroom are the curriculum and techniques of classroom management.

MORAL EDUCATION IN THE CLASSROOM

The Curriculum

John Dewey has suggested that social studies should constitute the core of the curriculum [13]. Two important aspects of social studies—the study of cultural differences and the evaluation of the long-term effects and interrelationships of policy decisions—not only directly affect the child's moral development but also may influence society itself.

CULTURAL DIFFERENCES

Acquaintance with different groups of people occurs as a matter of course in schools serving immigrants. In many countries immigrants form a sizable minority of the labor force and include people of every possible race and skin color, speaking a multitude of languages and living according to widely varying customs. In the United States, Switzerland, and Germany, for instance, where this is the case, many children meet people who seem very different from those in their own families. This situation can be used to acquaint the child with the different cultures. The child may learn first about the various products of the unfamiliar culture. Depending on the composition of the neighborhood, he may become acquainted with the taste of a tortilla, or the movement and emotion of a Greek dance, or a Chinese painting, or a black myth. But he must learn more. He must acquire knowledge, which is basic to mutual understanding, about the joys, the fears, and the aspirations of others.

He should be informed about the struggles and achievements of other people whose children he meets, about the difficulties of raising crops in the dry highlands of Mexico, for example, of the ocean trade and ancient sculptures of the Greeks, of the moral tenets of the Chinese, or the artistic and industrial triumphs of the Japanese. If he has contact with Jewish children, he can learn about the agricultural achievements of the Israelis. If he meets a Puerto Rican neighbor, he can learn about the importance of sugar cane for Puerto Rican economy.

If a school is situated in a racially and culturally uniform neighborhood, means should be used to acquaint children with different cultural groups. These could involve excursions and visits to other parts of the city, to other communities, or to other schools; arrangements could be made for visits from children or adults of other cultures; movies and music of other cultures could be presented at school. There are many ways that educators can introduce children to the culture of those different from them.

As Margaret Mead has described it, the goal of moral education in the United States at the beginning of the century was the education of the "homogenized" good American citizen that every immigrant was supposed to become [14]. In recent years a change of attitude has taken place. Now the value for an individual to maintain his cultural identity and for society to foster a rich diversity is acknowledged. The goal is no longer to homogenize the various cultures. At least on paper, the different cultures are accepted as equal.

As children learn about other cultures, their mutual understanding increases, hopefully bringing a changed attitude toward the populations in its wake. Moreover, children who feel secure in their own identity and traditions have greater potential for appreciating and accepting the cultures of others.

Jerome Bruner [15,16,17] among others, has discussed the role of social studies in developing an exploring and accepting attitude. When problem solving is based on information and discussion concerning human affairs, the child becomes prepared to think about how mankind can be influenced to strive toward a more secure future for all. Bruner suggested such topics as the bitter struggle of the Eskimos with their environment, the universal themes of myths, or how a child comes into being and how he develops. These approaches to learning about human needs and experiences may well change a child's attitude toward all members of the human race. Although for younger children the introduction of social studies is most helpful if it is based on direct contact with other cultures, audiovisual aids can be used when this is not possible.

SOCIAL PLANNING

People must learn to think through what they are planning so that they develop the necessary foresight. This is what Hersey and Blanchard called knowledge [18]. Critical understanding must be developed in children because many of the best intentions of social reformers give rise to projects that bring about the opposite of the desired results. A dam is built to provide water for irrigation—and other areas are deprived of water; a factory is built—and a river is polluted; dried milk is sent to Africa—and the children to whom it is fed become severely ill because they lack the necessary enzyme to digest it. All of us need to develop what might be called *multivariate social visualization;* that is, the ability to envisage various possible outcomes of a social act, to be flexible, to take into account the interrelationship of many relevant factors.

Such long-range, multifaceted evaluation of social policy requires intelligent, disinterested curiosity and research on the part of the teacher; it also demands a high degree of moral courage. Evaluation and discovery of interrelationships means going beyond the accepted wisdom of textbooks and authorities. But only by doing so will children imbibe the very essence of democratic thought.

Individualized Education and Morality

No education can be moral education if it does not respect each individual; such respect is the basis of both democracy and morality. It is the teacher's obligation to help each child to obtain the kind of education for which that particular child is best suited. The child also has a right to know that every effort is being made to provide this help.

Respect for the individual child as it is expressed in evaluation, choice of teaching methods, and techniques of classroom management have been discussed throughout this book. Certainly education, if it is to be moral, must concern itself with taking into account each child's individual interests and strengths and weaknesses. In short, *only effective, personalized education is moral education.*

Interrelationships among the Children

Another important approach to moral education is to change the behavior of the children in the natural environment of the classroom. The teacher can foster close contacts among the children and give them ample opportunities to interact freely and engage in common tasks. The teacher should use every means to promote a friendly atmosphere; for example, the teacher can ensure that he or she gives approval whenever a child is friendly toward another child, helps a peer, acknowledges a classmate's achievement. Hostility and competition should be minimized. Any tendency on the part of the children to form "in" groups and to be hostile to newcomers should be opposed, and a hospitable attitude toward any child entering the class should be fostered. An antisocial trend in some school-rooms that has to be checked is the assignment by the children of the role of the scapegoat to one or several of their classmates. The teacher must use influence to insure that this does not happen. The teacher should also be alert for the "loner" in the classroom and help such a child to be integrated into the group or to find a friend.

The teacher's role in creating a classroom environment favorable to positive social interaction is exemplified in research by Marion Yarrow and her co-workers who studied the relationships among environmental factors and the occurrence of sharing, comforting, and helping behaviors in children between the ages of 3 and 7½ [19]. They pointed out that although greater capacity for empathy developed with age, children also became more sensitive to the role of individual achievement and competition. Whether they responded in a caring manner to another's needs thus depended on the balance of these and other factors such as the children's expectations of adult and peer approval for doing so, the prohibitions they had learned (e.g., don't bother a crying person), the level of personal anxiety engendered by another's distress, and individual self-concept. Classroom experiences obviously exert a powerful influence on the development of these factors.

Interrelationships with Adults

As important as peer relationships are for the normal psychological development of the child, children should also have contact with adults. Urie Bronfenbrenner deplores the tendency to push children into a peer culture without permitting sufficient contact with other age groups [20].

The formation of gangs, with all the familiar deleterious side effects, is one of the results of age segregation. Another is the lack of respect for adults. After all, how can children respect adults when they know so few intimately? And how can they form life goals when they know so little about adult life? This is another reason why the school should undertake to acquaint the children with the customs, the work, the life, and the aspirations of adults from many walks of life. Parents, of course, can be very helpful in this respect. When Danny's father visits the class and tells the children about a building-trade union and Germaine's about the working of a bank, the children may get a deeper understanding not only of these social institutions, but also about Danny's pride in being the son of a man who "built a skyscraper" and Germaine's interest in savings accounts.

Human contacts are the basis for getting along with others; they are the basis for learning to trust and to like a variety of people and to be helpful to them. Thus, living may become more peaceful, and the rancor arising from racial, religious, cultural, language, and social differences may diminish. Is education not to a great extent learning about, understanding, and appreciating people?

Children should not only lose a negative attitude toward the people they meet but also gain a positive one, a commitment toward others. For this purpose they should become acquainted with the work of volunteers, the work of charitable organizations, and the tasks of the helping professions.

Classroom Activities

Changes of understanding and of attitude should finally lead to appropriate activities. Children can become involved in charitable work as well as in other activities that serve the community, the nation, and other countries. They can plan for collection of reusable materials, make footpaths for hikers, raise money for charities, or watch small children without asking for pay.

Such activities may be the first step in making the children aware of the needs common to our species, such as the protection of natural resources, the care of those in need, the need for recreation and healthful living, and above all, the need for planning. If these purposes are discussed with the children and exemplified by appropriate activities, then the school will contribute greatly to preparing the children to attain the worldwide outlook that is necessary for survival.

The Person of the Teacher

Children's behavior tends to reflect the teacher's characteristics. The teacher is one of the most important modeling agents for the child. Albert Bandura reports that modeling affects such diverse behaviors as response style, self-evaluation, delay of gratification, and moral judgment [21].

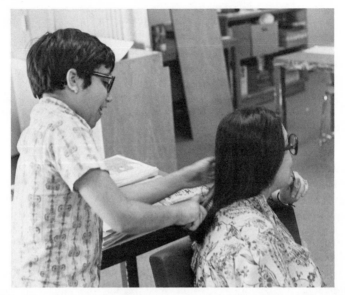

Fig. 11-1.   A caring teacher finds that her students also show caring behavior: This young man knew that his teacher always brought her hairbrush, and during recess he decided to explore the role of hairdresser. (Photo by James Quinn and Michael Campa.)

The philosopher and writer Julian Huxley stated that self-restraint is the essence of the ethical process [22]. Self-restraint is not easily achieved, but it is a necessary characteristic of the teacher who aspires to include an education toward a new ethic into the curriculum. When a teacher suggests that the children should learn to subordinate their own needs for the common good, the same teacher must demonstrate by his or her own behavior a willingness to do the same. The teacher may thus prevent the children from growing up with the purely hedonistic attitude that so many people exhibit.

The Efficacy of Moral Instruction

Almost everyone desires to bring about a higher level of moral development, but many people feel that morality is not something that can be taught as such.

A study by M. J. Chandler disputes this conclusion [23]. He studied 45 delinquent boys and 45 nondelinquent boys between the ages of 11 and 13. Both groups were first given a test of flexible empathy; the delinquents made more than three times as many errors as the nondelinquents. The delinquents were then divided into three groups. The first group met for half a day per week for ten weeks to make films that emphasized awareness of other viewpoints and relationships among these points of view and in which each boy had to play all the roles. The second group made films that did not involve the boys directly; and the third group served as control. The group trained in role-taking made significantly higher scores on a post-test of empathy. In the follow-up 18 months later, it was found that the frequency of arrest for the trained group was down by almost half. More research and curriculum development in this area certainly seem warranted.

MORAL EDUCATION AND EDUCATIONAL ORGANIZATION

Staff Interrelationships

It is most important that the members of the school staff be united in trying to include moral education into the curriculum. A single member of the educational staff, whether a teacher, a psychologist, or an administrator, cannot bring about much change. The school as a whole must become pervaded with a spirit of cooperation. Schools do exist that are characterized by an atmosphere of freedom and lack of anxiety, which are the basis of all effective education. In England the author observed such schools in Oxfordshire and shared the enjoyment and excitement in learning that was evident in all of the classrooms.* The close cooperation of the staff was obvious. The school was a beehive of activities. The children were vertically grouped and could freely move to other groups. The teachers as well as the children supplied each other with ideas. The school seemed to belong to the children, and the children seemed to feel happy and at home.

Teachers who like to work in such an atmosphere may only be able to extend it initially to their own classroom, but such a venture may be the first step in changing the atmosphere of the school to one in which enthusiasm in working together on the part of both children and teachers prevails. When the administrators become interested, then the process may be accelerated. Whoever is the initiator has to be aware that much initial planning with other staff members may be necessary, and all possible effort should be exerted to establish the same friendly atmosphere among the staff as reigns among the children.

The Role of Research

Research workers have only indirect contact with the classroom, but their influence is great. Research in philosophy, biology, child development,

*See also, for example, the description of such schools in *Crisis in the Classroom* by Silberman [2].

psychology, and sociology is all relevant for education. The teacher must use much time for study; even more important is that the teacher must learn to read critically. Much so-called "research" has been done more for the glory of the writer than for the benefit of the children. On the other hand, findings of significant value for educational purposes may lie hitherto unnoticed or unapplied, until an alert educator recognizes its significance.

The relationship of research to education should not be a one-way street. The most crucial educational research must be done in the classroom. Therefore, the teacher has to play an important part, especially in relation to the understanding of the individual children. Research based on group averages, which today is too often the preferred approach, does not tell much about the individual child. There are many children who react differently from the majority. How can we educate these children? How can we assist those who have difficulties in adjusting to their environment and are hazards for themselves and others? On the other hand, how can we develop the abilities of those children who may be able to find solutions for some aspects of the current human predicament? How can we educate leaders? All these are essentially questions of applied morality.

Another problem in regard to research is its use in the classroom. There are aspects of education on which researchers of different persuasions and fields of knowledge agree, and still the classroom teacher does not act as these findings indicate. Not to act on the basis of the best available information is immoral.

For example, it is well-known that children learn best through activity. Both Montessori and Dewey wanted children to be active. The research of Piaget and many neurophysiologists—for example, N. Bernstein [24], D. O. Hebb [25], and K. H. Pribram [26]—shows the importance of experience and activity in education, and a great host of writers (as a matter of fact, practically everybody who has been interested in child development) discuss the importance of the interactions of children in play as well as in work. Yet there are still many classrooms in which the children are hardly permitted to move. That imaginative play may be an important aspect of education "even" after kindergarten is still seen as heresy by many educators.

Another influence adverse to the optimum benefit of research findings is that much research is often misunderstood or misapplied. Both Dewey and Montessori were concerned with social goals in education and with the teaching methods, classroom structure, and curricula that might lead to these goals, but their contributions have been grossly misunderstood and misused and their ideas distorted.

Montessori [27] suggested that the social awareness of children would be enhanced if they participated in the management of the classroom. Nevertheless, modern followers of Montessori often forget that this communal work was to be done in a spirit of mutual helpfulness. In addition to describing her excellent teaching aids and their use, Montessori also emphasized that in the classroom there be a spirituality, joy in living, appreciation of beauty, creativity, music and art, and an interest in moral questions. Many Montessori schools are quite lacking in these characteristics and run precisely counter to the spirit of the great Dotoressa.

The writings of most great leaders in education have discussed the interrelationships of the various aspects of education: how the curriculum should be presented as well as the nature of its content, classroom management, the appropriate behavior of the children toward each other, the leadership role of the teacher. The great educators and researchers in education discussed such factors as they relate to each other; but too often a teacher or administrator will seize upon only one aspect of given research and therefore distort it and apply it wrongly. Dewey's teachings again provide an example. Curriculum designers have sometimes imposed on children specific subject matter for which they were not prepared in order to follow a particular lead of Dewey's.

The author remembers being told when teaching in a rural inland southwestern elementary school that *all* third-grade children *always* love to study boats because *all* 8-year-old children are interested in boats. I asked my supervisor, "But what should I do if these children should be more interested in Mexico? There are many Mexican children in the class and most of them have never seen a lake or ocean." "Oh," said the superior, "just put pictures of boats in the classroom and nothing else, then they will ask about boats." Dewey [28] himself had to write a book to contradict the misuses of his doctrines and practices.

It is true that misunderstanding of research can occur in good faith, but the frequent attacks on valuable research are not always done in good faith. Peters rightly notes,

> I have constantly been astonished in academic life about the extent to which reputations depend on fashion. "Oh, he's no good," it is said. But try probing for the evidence on which such judgements are based, and note how often they are made by people who have never read the man's work, heard him lecture, or anything like that. [6, p 110]

Much research whose application could be helpful is lost in this way. A negative or skeptical attitude, like any other attitude, is justified only if it is based on knowledge and understanding. The moral educator makes every effort to read widely, intensively, and critically.

MORAL EDUCATION, THE COMMUNITY, THE LARGER SOCIETY

Relationship with Parents and Community

The main task of the teacher is to educate the children, but the cooperation of society in reaching ethical goals is indispensable in a democracy, and especially in a democracy in which the population is so highly diversified as it is in the United States. Educators must listen to the voices of the inner city, the blacks, the whites, the middle-class suburbans, the rural poor, and the well-to-do farmers. They must listen to the Puerto Ricans, to the Chinese, to the Mexicans, to the American Indians, and to many other groups. Each group has its own wishes and concerns. In communicating with all these various people, we have to take their opinions respectfully into account while keeping in mind the goal of an ethical education.

To reach these objectives, it is crucial that all teachers continually remind themselves that modeling is an all-important educational practice and that this applies to contacts with the parents as well as with the children. An open, friendly, and positive attitude will play a large part in providing mutual cooperation. Willingness to extend oneself, idealism, enthusiasm, courage, and empathy may change the attitudes of the community, especially if these qualities pervade the whole school staff.

First, the staff must be ready to alleviate the anxieties of the parents with respect to their children's learning, the school program, and the discipline; and they must allay the anxiety of the community concerning the value of the goals set up for the children. As with the children, educators must establish mutual trust before we can be effective with the parents and with the community as a whole. We must be skillful in explaining our goals. We must make our professional integrity manifest and demonstrate both our skills and our eagerness to help the children; we must demonstrate our caring.

We should not disparage the use of parental "M and Ms" in the form of pleasurable activities for the parents, such as arranging for a performance of the children or an exhibition of their work, or inviting the parents to a discussion group led by a psychologist or another member of the educational staff, or sending a congratulatory note concerning the achievements of a child or group of children, or having an article published about the PTA's marvelous work in the local newspaper. Publicity is always an effective tool because it is flattering to most people. All of these measures will help to establish a closer bond with the community, with the parents, and with the children.

Educators should also support organizations that unify the community, such as Hot Line or other volunteer services or committees for festivities. All organizational activities that bring the members of the community together for a worthwhile purpose may be instrumental in supporting the educational facilities.

Small steps are necessary to prepare the community for thinking on a bigger scale. It cannot be overemphasized that mutual trust must be established before educators can expect a freer hand to educate children so that they can also learn to trust each other, their fellow citizens, and those of other nations, and finally so that they can learn to forego pleasure when the common need warrants it. The cooperation of the community is needed for *all* aspects of education, not only for moral education. The teacher has to prove mastery of the task of educating the children and respect for the wishes of the community in regard to the aims of the educational process, whether academic, vocational, or technical.

The school staff is not the only agency educating the children. The parents, the Scout master, the priest, and other influential people in the community, as well as the street gangs, peers, and siblings, influence the behavior of children. These influences may guide the child in different directions than the school. Therefore, it is necessary to communicate with these agencies—not only those agencies that are willing to help but also those that resist. It has been demonstrated, for example, that it is possible to convince street gangs and clubs that the school is doing its best to act in the best interests of the children.

As far as the parents are concerned, they are nearly always glad to receive guidance in relation to educating their children. They also need a forum where they can express their grievances so as to become more insightful in relation to their own feelings. Skillful and thoughtful teachers and school administrators pay equal attention to parents of every background as well as to significant members of the community. These same school personnel strive to guide parents and befriend them and in so doing change their attitudes constructively. It is astonishing to see former hostile human beings suddenly derive great joy from what we may call ''doing the right thing.''

What counts most in promoting change are ideas and ideals, and our ideas and ideals must be shared with children, with society, and with our fellow educators. The educational staff must talk to clerks, unions, lodges, parents, friends, and enemies. In furthering the aim of introducing a moral education, however, we must also try to convince our fellow Americans, whenever we feel that the idea is not too shocking, that we must think in global terms, in terms that encompass not only this nation but all of humanity. At least we must try to convey that what happens in our corner of the globe may affect all mankind and that today's ethics, therefore, must be concerned with the needs of all who live on this earth. Underlying this concern with communication is the assumption that the educational staff itself truly values all of humanity and respects and marvels at human achievement everywhere, present as well as past. Only then can there be hope for introducing and furthering moral behavior.

Social Conscience and the School

The environmental changes wrought by technology have been so rapid and so far-reaching that the adaptation of society as a whole, as well as of the majority of individuals, has lagged further and further behind. The result is an all-pervading anxiety. The young, especially, are plagued by doubt and uncertainty and mistrust. They cannot foresee how they will master their own fate after they become adults. Often they have little energy left for transcendent emotions and for a caring attitude toward their fellow man. In regard to striving after ideals, they often even do not know what to strive for. A school atmosphere that helps the child to gain trust is, therefore, the basis for any ethical education. The influence of the school cannot be decisive, however, when the child lives in an environment that destroys or prevents establishment of trust and hope.

Particularly since the 1950s an enormous amount of evidence has been accumulated in the United States and elsewhere about conditions that hamper a child's development and the conditions that enhance it. The damaging evidence of poverty has become increasingly evident. Poverty-stricken children do not live in an atmosphere that develops trust; physical impairment may be added to the emotional damage of such an atmosphere. A child's development and learning ability may be affected by malnutrition of the pregnant mother, malnutrition of the infant, lack of stimulation, unsanitary conditions, and an atmosphere of strife or worry or despair.

It is certainly an important task of the school to explain the dangers of poverty to the public and hopefully be instrumental in getting remedial measures instituted. It is acknowledged that each child in America has a right to education, and educational facilities are provided for almost every child. The school has been charged with the responsibility of educating each child to the limits of his or her capacities. But the education of a child whose brain has been damaged because of malnutrition or poor hygienic conditions will be impaired. A child who is hungry cannot learn. The school, because it is directly concerned and because it believes in the moral principles that it teaches, can and must take responsibility and provide leadership to ensure that adequate medical care and nutrition is available to all.

The school must also educate the community to the consequences of unemployment. "The best-kept secret in America today is that people would rather work hard for something they believe in than enjoy a pampered idleness" [29, p. 148]. When the idleness is not "pampered," as it usually is not during unemployment, hopelessness becomes overwhelming. It is important for the American public to understand the psychological as well as the economic disruption that unemployment causes. Unemployment not only causes poverty, it also makes life meaningless and destroys the spirit as well as the body. The young child of a family that imminently expects or experiences unemployment may be damaged by the adults' uncertainty and despair; the adolescent, by the fear of not finding work after he will leave school.

In summary, educators must become more keenly aware of inadequacies and dysfunctioning in the social system and must develop their own social conscience as well as the awareness and social conscience of the children and of society as a whole.

CONCLUSION

There is still hope for a better future, but not unless the majority of people learn that it is necessary to subordinate their own pleasure to their ideals and beliefs and that the necessities of life must be more equally distributed on a worldwide scale. We believe in equal rights for all, but what rights have the unemployed, what rights have the hungry, what rights have the poor who come into conflict with the law, what rights has the poor child who dies because a physician's help is not available, or what rights has the mother who has to leave her child in order to go to work?

Our future is only safe if human beings do not feel powerlessly condemned to misery or satisfied while others are miserable. Gross injustice paves the way for a dictator or for violent revolution, or maybe even for the destruction of this earth.

Our circumstances require the birth of a new ethics that is not built on fear of punishment or on hope for personal reward but on a code of ethics that is anchored in the inner conviction that not only does immoral behavior lead ultimately to our doom but that there is joy in doing what one may call "the right thing"—that this is in fact the natural attitude when it is encouraged to flower.

REFERENCES

1. Erikson EH: Dimensions of a New Identity. New York, W. W. Norton, 1974
2. Silberman C: Crisis in the Classroom. New York, Random House, 1971
3. Platt JR: The Skinnerian revolution, in Wheeler H (ed): Beyond the Punitive Society. San Francisco, Freeman, 1973
4. Monod J: Le hasard et la nécessité. Paris, Editions du Seuil, 1970
5. Borke H: Interpersonal perception of young children. Dev Psychol 5: 263–269, 1971
6. Peters RS: Authority, Responsibility, and Education (ed 3). London, Allen & Unwin, 1973
7. Fishbein HD: Evolution, Development, and Children's Learning. Pacific Palisades, Calif., Goodyear, 1976
8. Feffer M: Developmental analysis of interpersonal behavior. Psychol Rev 77:197–214, 1970
9. Selman RL, Byrne DF: A structural-developmental analysis of levels of role taking in middle childhood. Child Dev 45:803–806, 1974
10. Piaget J: The Moral Judgment of the Child. New York, Free Press, 1965
11. Kohlberg L, Gilligan C: The adolescent as a philosopher. Daedalus, 28, 162–215, 1971
12. Damon W: Early conceptions of positive justice as related to the development of logical operations. Child Dev. 46: 301–312, 1975
13. Dewey J: Early Works, 1889–1892. Carbondale, Southern Illinois University Press, 1969
14. Mead M: The school in American cultures, abstract in Halsey AH, Floud JE,

Anderson CA (eds): Education, Economy and Society. New York, Free Press, 1961

15. Bruner JS: On going beyond the information given, in Contemporary Approaches to Cognition. Cambridge, Harvard University Press, 1957
16. Bruner JS: The Process of Education. Cambridge, Harvard University Press, 1960
17. Bruner JS: The art of discovery. Harv Ed Rev 3: 21–32, 1961
18. Hersey P, Blanchard KH: Management of Organizational Behavior (ed 2). Englewood Cliffs, N.J., Prentice-Hall, 1972
19. Yarrow MR, Waxler CZ, in collaboration with Barrett D, Darby J, King R, Pickett M, Smith J: Dimensions and correlates of prosocial behavior in young children. Child Dev: 47:118–125, 1976
20. Bronfenbrenner U: Two Worlds of Childhood. New York, Russell Sage Foundation, 1970
21. Bandura A: Principles of Behavior Modification. New York, Holt, 1969
22. Huxley J: Touchstone for Ethics. New York, Harper & Row, 1971
23. Chandler MJ: Egocentrism and anti-social behavior: the assessment and training of social perspective-taking skills. Dev Psychol 9:326–333, 1973
24. Bernstein N: The Coordination and Regulation of Movement. New York, Pergamon, 1967
25. Hebb DO: Organization of Behavior. New York, Wiley, 1949
26. Pribram KH: Languages of the Brain. Englewood Cliffs, N.J., Prentice-Hall, 1971
27. Montessori M: The Montessori Method. New York, Schocken, 1964
28. Dewey J: Experience and Education. New York, Collier, 1938
29. Gardner JW: Excellence, Can We Be Equal and Excellent Too? New York, Harper & Row, 1961

Afterword

The technological, social, and economic changes of our time offer great opportunities for self-development, but at the same time they threaten our very survival. Technology has provided many people with greater leisure; it has also provided weaponry that can destroy in a moment large portions of the world and its population. It has provided extraordinary material comforts for masses of people; and it has brought about a drastic depletion in the world's resources, violation of its natural beauties, and pollution of earth, air, and water. Urbanization has "freed" people from dependence on the land for survival—and thrust millions into asphalt jungles, slums, and ghettos where normal human needs for movement, space, privacy, clean air, natural beauty, and a relationship with nature are suppressed.

Education has the responsibility of helping all of our children to fulfill their individual potential. At the same time it must prepare them to deal with the problems of our era and to consider future generations in their actions. It must enable them to develop communicative and technical skills to the utmost to learn to think and to act creatively and with forethought rather than mechanically, to acquire a social conscience that is global in scope rather than parochially bounded, and to develop the sensitivity and compassion upon which the quality of the personal life and the only human progress that is worthwhile depend.

In our time ugliness, anxiety, loneliness, violence, and exploitation threaten us all. Humanistic strivings, nevertheless, are evident the world over. More people are showing concern about the ravages of war, hunger, and pollution and the unbridled materialism which tends to foster these conditions.

There is a reawakening of interest in folk art, music, and crafts, and many are attempting to lead lives based on simplicity and beauty rather than competitive striving. Enormous effort, however, is needed to counteract the negative forces of our time. There is no Aladdin's lamp to rub and make of our dreams an instant reality.

Instead, we who are educators must use all of our awareness and creativity to lead children in a patient step-by-step progression toward the mutual tolerance, understanding, and friendship as well as refinement of thought, feelings, and skills that the world so badly needs.

As educators we will be greatly rewarded in this endeavor, even though we know that the educational goals that have been outlined in this book cannot be fully realized without changes in the attitude of society toward education.

Teachers will have greater enthusiasm if they feel adequately rewarded not only in terms of salary but especially in terms of support from authorities. Like their students, teachers should have the benefit of the inner satisfactions to be derived from exercising their own ideas and innovations without feeling too closely inhibited by rigid requirements imposed from above. Teachers need to respect the individuality and creativity of their children. Their own individuality and creativity also need to be respected. Given these conditions, teachers will approach their task with greater confidence and enthusiasm, and they will more often and more amply exemplify Chaucer's description of the good educator: "And gladly wolde he lerne and gladly teche."

A word is needed about the teacher's self-development in a broader sense. A teacher's education is not only a matter of keeping up with the latest ideas about and techniques of teaching but also of cultivating the whole person in the same way that we try to take into account the whole child. The best transmitter of a culture is one who is himself cultured; of an ethical attitude, one who is himself ethical; of respect and compassion, one who is himself respectful and compassionate; of an enthusiasm for learning, one who is himself such an enthusiast; of an appreciation for beauty, one who loves what is beautiful himself; and of creativity, one who is himself creative. In these respects our education never ends. And if we sometimes need inspiration, we could not do better than try to emulate the qualities that we so often find in the children who are our charge.

Index

a
b
c
6 d
7 e
8 f
9 g
0 h
1 i
8 2 j